Images of Violence

Responding to children's representations of the violence they see

Siân Adams and
Janet Moyles

Published by Featherstone Education Ltd
PO Box 6350
Lutterworth
LE17 6ZA

First published March 2005
Text © Siân Adams and Janet Moyles, 2005
Publication © Featherstone Education

Project Management & Design: Phill Featherstone
Editing: Phill Featherstone, Vicky Smith
Illustrations: Kerry Ingham
Photographs (except right hand picture on p90) by the authors

ISBN 1 905019 15 7

Message from the publisher
We have been unable to trace the owners of the copyright of the photograph printed on p90. If the copyright owner would contact us we will be pleased to make appropriate arrangements.

Featherstone
Education

Printed in the UK on paper produced in the European Union from
managed, sustainable forests

Images of Violence

Resp... ...dre... representations of the violence ...

The Authors

Siân Adams has extensive experience of teaching young children in Key Stage 1 and the Foundation Stage. Following her time in schools, she was an advisory teacher for early years, which involved her in work in schools and several universities in the Midlands. This combination of working with children and practitioners in different educational settings and within academic institutions provided the opportunity to link principles with practice, bringing both into sharp relief. An interest in exploring practitioners' reflective thinking was developed during her PhD at Leicester University. During this period she worked with Janet Moyles, pursuing a range of research projects which further investigated the ways in which practitioners confronted the many pedagogical dilemmas encountered in their work with young children. Recently retired, Siân now explores the delights of young children's responses with her own grandchildren!

Janet Moyles is Emeritus Professor of Education at Anglia Polytechnic University and an early years consultant. She has a PhD from the University of Leicester, which explored the ideologies and beliefs of early years practitioners. She began her career and interest in young children through the playgroup movement and her own two sons, eventually deciding to train as a teacher. She taught in several schools before becoming a headteacher, after which the academic life beckoned. Janet has directed several funded research projects and published widely on issues related to early years practices, especially play and practitioner roles. It is her opinion that play, in all its forms, is still not well understood by either practitioners or the general public. This is especially true of any form of play which involves adults' perceptions of 'violence'.

Foreword

This deeply thoughtful and thought-provoking book acknowledges the demanding and painful human issues which face us all now that media images of violence and war are so pervasive and powerful. The authors draw on their long experience of observing children and training early years practitioners, and relate this to theory and research evidence. They refer to principles underpinning children's rights to show how reflective practitioners can help each other, and the diverse children, families and communities with whom they work, in coming to terms with disturbing experiences.

At some level, each of us has been forced to confront our own fears and uncertainties about recent events worldwide, and the way they are reported. Easy assumptions are not an option as the need to redouble informed efforts to foster children's personal, social and moral development becomes painfully evident. The cameos reported here express the feelings of real people in recognisable situations. They demand, and are granted, honest discussion that does not trivialise or gloss over reality, or ignore children's authentic concerns. There are no simple answers, but ways forward are illustrated through the process of genuine debate. We owe it to future generations to engage with the challenges presented so clearly in this book.

Wendy Scott

Acknowledgements

The authors acknowledge with gratitude the help, information, inspiration and advice of members of the Early Years Curriculum Group (EYCG), who provided the initial inspiration to research this topic. Those involved (in alphabetical order) were: Sally Barnes, Bernadette Duffy, Margaret Edgington, Julie Fisher, Andrew Lockett, Linda Pound, Dorothy Selleck, Wendy Scott and Pauline Trudell. We are particularly indebted to Wendy for writing the Foreword.

We are also grateful for the support of The Vicky Hurst Trust in the development of this publication.

We take full responsibility for the opinions expressed in this document and offer them in an effort to stimulate thinking and discussion on these very sensitive issues.

Note:
By the term 'practitioner' we mean any adult working with young children in whatever setting. Where an individual has a specific designation, e.g. teacher, this is used in place of practitioner.

Contents

Images of Violence

Introduction

On the morning of September 11th, 2001, two airliners came out of a cloudless sky to crash into the twin towers of the World Trade Centre. The images of that terrible event, which within minutes appeared on television screens all over the world, had a unique impact. Many people have remarked that the unfolding catastrophe looked more like a disaster movie than real life. Individual and mass tragedies were beamed into millions of homes. Key images appeared again and again, firstly as news bulletins reporting the happenings and then as material for lengthy and detailed analyses. Television also reflected the responses of those who witnessed or heard about the disaster: shock, anger, horror, heartbreak from many, but also triumph and exultation from some.

Play is the means children use to process and understand their experience of the world around them. Practitioners know this very well. They also know from their own experience and observation how frequently this play includes elements of violence. There is an extensive literature on this, a significant portion of which is referred to in this book.

However, although used to encountering elements of violence in children's play, for many early years practitioners the happenings of September 11th, and others that followed them - such as the Bali and Madrid bombings, created new challenges. Echoes of these violent events soon made an appearance in children's play. Media coverage highlighted and brought into sharper focus the underlying difficulties of rationalising and defining ways of responding to children's perceptions and representations of violence. This is an issue whenever and however children react to the images of violence they see. It is particularly true of events that have elements of shock and surprise, which are characteristics of terrorism, and which therefore immediately become high profile news items. Practitioners need to consider and establish ways of responding to young children's reactions to violent events such as these, and their representations of what we define later as 'cultural violence'.

Images of Violence

Before we come to definitions we need to appreciate the impact the images we shall discuss can have on the mind of a child. A good place to begin is by reminding ourselves of the effect that media coverage of terrorist atrocities can have on us as adults. For example:

- Where were you on September 11th? (This is something you'll probably never forget.)

- How did the images you saw of what was happening in the USA make you feel?

One of the authors was working at her desk when a friend telephoned and urged her to turn on the television. She did so and wondered why the caller was telling her to look at what as far as she could see was a disaster movie. This initial reaction was soon replaced by the awesome realisation that in reality this was no movie; it was something far more serious. A variety of emotions followed in rapid succession: horror, outrage, distress, disbelief, anger, sadness… similar reactions, no doubt, to those experienced by many of us.

It is understandable that the response of many parents and practitioners was to avoid, and even suppress, any mention or discussion of the September 11th events with children. There are, of course, plenty of reasons for this. For example, many practitioners want to protect young minds and emotions from images and experiences which could be very disturbing.

The attack on the World Trade Centre is sadly by no means unique in the sorry chronicle of world horror. From the blanket bombing of civilians in World War II to the meticulous genocide of Rwanda, there is no shortage of examples of human-kind's capacity for violence. What was different about September 11th was an almost unique element of shock. Here was an attack on the heartland of the USA – hitherto apparently invulnerable to such things. This was combined with an intimacy and immediacy rarely seen before. The assassination of President Kennedy comes to mind as, perhaps, one of the few other violent events that one can remember being played and replayed on the televison in such infinite and painstaking detail. On September 11th, as rarely before, millions of us saw the violence unfold before our eyes, carried into our own homes and places of work. The events which followed September 11th seemed to nudge the media reporting of violence on to a new and different level. 21st century terrorism was different.

Soon after September 11th we started to observe some new elements in children's play. These appeared to be directly related to what they had seen in the media. When we discussed this with other practitioners we found that they shared our perception. Children seemed to be struggling to find a response to these different violent images, and they were doing so as they always have, through their play. The case studies which begin each of the focus points all come from the observations we made at that time. The issue we all faced as practitioners was how best to respond to children's reactions to these images of violence.

There are other aspects of September 11th which also have a bearing on our consideration of its impact on children. For example, although there was incredible destruction, there were few visible casualties. This added to the sense of unreality many felt as they watched, and combined with the vividness of the images to give what was happening the appearance of fiction (we have already noted Siân's confusion when first turning on the 9/11 news coverage). How was this event, which was clearly having such an impact on adults, different for many children from what they had seen in the last video rental? Secondly, the perpetrators were anonymous. Although everyone knew who was being attacked, it was not clear by whom. The normal polarisation of 'baddies' and 'goodies' that is common in children's comic books and television programmes was absent. So was the catharsis which comes from seeing the triumph of good over evil. Besides, just *who* were the baddies and *who* were the goodies? The adult world, usually so precise in matters of right and wrong, was not clear about this. Juxtaposed with the devastation of people and property in New York were images of crowds celebrating in Palestine.

Images of Violence

Another feature which we must mention in considering the media reporting of this new terrorism; that is the racism, particularly the anti-Muslim sentiment, embedded within the narrative of broadcasters and commentators describing 9/11. This has also been apparent in the reporting of other acts of terrorism and in the coverage of action against terrorists in the Middle East, and is a particular issue for settings in mixed race and multi-cultural populations. Such racial and cultural elements have driven rifts through many communities and even families. Children from different cultural and racial heritages bring their varied experiences of adult views and responses into the settings they attend. They do not always sit comfortably with those of the practitioners who teach them.

For many of us working in mixed communities the weeks, months and years since September 11th have thrown up huge challenges which are no easier with the passage of time. It has become increasingly difficult for them to determine how to address the anxieties and confusion amongst the young children they observe in their settings in ways appropriate to their development and cultures. Many strong feelings have surfaced, and views have polarized to the extent that they threaten to split societies across the world and undermine the progress which has been made towards multiracial harmony and understanding.

September 11th has become for early years practitioners the catalyst for an exploration of pedagogical responses to issues that arise when children are exposed to extensive violence in the media. For example, one can see almost daily on television news abundant evidence of war, terrorism, famine and death. But what is war to one person, is a 'jihad' to another: what is terrorism to some is to others a justifiable – perhaps, as they see it, the only – means of achieving an end. Young children are aware of this and involved in it through the behaviour of the adults in their lives. In an effort to understand it they will play out what they see and bring into their settings the ideas and views they heave heard expressed.

Early years practitioners agree on the value to children of playing out real life as a means of understanding and coming to terms with what they see and experience in the world outside. In order to support and stimulate role play, schools and settings try to emulate the outside world for children by offering home areas and make believe buses, aeroplanes, shops, and so on. For decades practitioners have deliberated the rights and wrongs of encouraging, condoning, excluding or ignoring children's gun and weapon play: cops and robbers, superheroes, cowboys and indians or general rough and tumble. These issues have already been thoroughly explored (Smith and Lewis 1985; Blurton Jones 1972; Paley 1991). How much to permit or not to permit has been a recurring concern. Are children representing their perception of reality? Or are they fantasising? All agree on the importance of role play to child development. Is violent role play equally as valid and vital as playing out, say, a shopping trip or a visit to the doctor?

Parents and practitoners will confirm that violence is a particular feature of boys' play. Smith's research (2004a: 153) found that '...boys' play shows an integration of pretend ... with rough-and-tumble elements ... there is a story theme of sorts, but it shifts ... unlike domestic themes [such as in girls' play]'. This kind of socio-dramatic play is more fantastic, relying on stories, television and film. Girls tend towards less dramatic and more homely play.

The early years workforce is mainly female, and has often frowned upon rough-and-tumble, gun and weapon play in a basic feminine instinct to control representations of violence and steer children in directions they consider to be more creative and constructive. Increasingly practitioners are beginning to question their intuitive responses of *We don't have guns in school...* (or swords, arrows, zappers, light sabres or the myriad other pretend weapons many seem to want).

Guns are apparent every day on television and in other media. Isn't it natural for children to incorporate these into their play as part of their mechanism for processing and understanding the adult world? It is especially difficult to discourage violent and weapon play in a setting when it is tolerated or even encouraged at home. Many parents are 'manipulated by media, commercial and manufacturing interests to purchase and 'consume' [certain] toys' (Smith 1994; Sutton-Smith 1988). Whilst most parents appear not to like war play, Sutton-Smith (1988) found that for children it simply reflects an aspect of real life. As one boy in Sutton-Smith's research said when his father asked him not to use toy guns 'But Dad, I don't want to shoot anybody: I just want to play'!

Young children's reactions to the violent images and role models society places before them have tended to polarise concerns regarding exposure to violence and terrorism within UK culture (Kelly and Mullander 2000; Bruce and Meggitt 1999; Roberts 1995). Representations of terrorism and the hostilities evident in contemporary society are often observed in children's play, behaviour and language – and have been for as long as children's activities have been documented (Tephly 1985; Ariès 1962). Previous considerations regarding the provision of toy guns and swords, for example, have now developed into more weighty concerns as early years professionals face further dilemmas as a result of young children presenting the extent of their increasing awareness of violence around them in society.

In this book we present recent evidence that children's responses are becoming more personalised and may be accompanied by racist undertones; neither of these matters can be ignored (Lane 1999). We examine some of the instances which have been reported to us by practitioners of children incorporating into their art and play what they saw and heard immediately following and in the months since the traumatic events of September 11th 2001. Children have represented the violence in a number of ways, and practitioners are exploring what might be the most appropriate means of responding to these 'playful' examples of talk and behaviour which have such a disturbing content and context. This presents challenges for everyone who works in an early years setting (Hauge 2000), particularly for the many practitioners who themselves have little direct experience of violence, terrorism or racial conflict.

Consider the photograph below. It is a model of the twin towers. It was made by a four-year-old, whose name is Joseph. It shows how he sought to depict the image of the towers as he had experienced and understood it.

How would you have responded if Joseph had produced this construction in your school or setting?

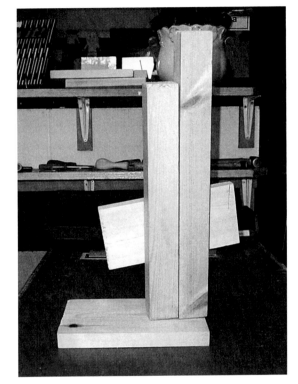

- Would you discuss the contents of his structure with Joseph?

- Would you ask questions? If so, what would you ask?

- Would you say anything to the other children? If so, what would you say?

- Would you discuss Joseph's model with his parents? How would you go about this?

- Would you discuss it with colleagues?

- Would you display Joseph's model of the twin towers in your setting?

- Would you encourage Joseph or other children to make other representations of this and similar images of violence?

- What professional knowledge and experience would you use to inform your responses to Joseph?

- Based on what you see here, can you form any view of Joseph's social or cultural background? Or of his prior learning?

- Would you respond differently if Joanne (rather than Joseph) had made this model? If so, how? And why?

- Consider the responsibility you have for children's emotional development, social development, moral development. In what ways do you teach children to take account of and respect the cultures and viewpoints of others?

- How can you discriminate between 'innocent' behaviour (e.g. creative use of building blocks) and other behaviour influenced by aspects of violence (e.g. gun play or violent games in the play area), so as to be alert to the danger of placing adult interpretations on or overreacting to behaviour which is a natural part of children's development?

And finally …

What personal responses are provoked in you as you consider these questions?

Discussions with your colleagues about Joseph's model are likely to reveal the diverse and contradictory emotional and cognitive responses by adults to the events of September 11th and other recent acts of violence and war. It is important to remember that in many ways these dilemmas are not new, or even unique to the 21st century. But they are more pressing now as children, as well as their parents, are saturated with the coverage of violent events through media which, because of advances in technology, have more power and effect than in the past. We now take for granted images seen on television, on the internet or in newspapers, and children today have greater exposure than ever before to images of violence. *Are we able to bring an informed educational understanding to the consideration of what children make of the images with which they are now continually surrounded?*

Children's representations of violence

The aim of this book is to identify some of the necessary pedagogical processes that practitioners may need to follow when they encounter children's responses to the reporting of terrorism. There is no easy prescription for reacting to such complex situations. Practitioners may well be involved in some difficult examinations of previously held personal beliefs and values. That will inevitably give rise to some challenging questions. These have to be faced in order to decide how best to support children.

This is the reason for the questions we raised earlier. Did they challenge you? Learning, real learning about ourselves and the issues which affect us, cannot take place without some discomfort (Claxton 1999). The authors and the early years experts consulted on this project know this from personal experience. From the outset of undertaking the background research for this book and delving into the issues ourselves, we have needed to debate and confront our own personal, cultural and professional values. At times this exploration has been a painful and difficult process. Defining personal values and questioning cherished beliefs and prejudices is uncomfortable and gives rise to feelings of vulnerability, insecurity and frustration. At times we have been surprised and perplexed at both our own feelings and the unexpected strengths of the views of some of our colleagues. There is a need to respect and value one another's differences as well as similarities.

The reality of this leads to a complex journey, difficult but valuable and satisfying. We have made no attempt to sanitise this process for our readers. Instead we offer a series of signposts, which aim to inform and empower their thinking and support their deliberations about the violent or potentially threatening situations with which we are frequently confronted. The references and bibliography on page 126 give a range of resources which can support practitioners in different ways. There is interesting evidence surrounding these issues in current literature, which can help to map possible ways forward. We hope that this book will assist readers by encouraging further critical reflection and informed discussion with colleagues, children and parents.

Firstly, however, we need to clarify what we mean in the context of our discussion by the terms 'culture' and 'cultural violence'. For the purposes of this book we have assumed the following :

Images of Violence

CULTURE refers to the attitudes and values current in a society or community. It is based on the perspectives, traditions and beliefs, shared by members of a particular community. Included in this are music, art, language, customs, etiquettes, rituals of politeness, celebrations and so on.

We use CULTURAL VIOLENCE to indicate the pervasive effects of violence emanating from the media, literature and values within children's families, cultures and the local community.

We have identified three key areas in our examination of children's and practitioners responses to violence and terrorism. These form the basis on which we set out to define and explore the ways young children represent what we have termed cultural violence, and the ways in which they respond to it, individually and collectively.

The three key areas are:

1. Media – the ways in which violence and terrorism are now communicated to young children;
2. Adults' reactions and responsibilities – at personal as well as professional levels;
3. Children's entitlements – to be enabled to explore through play and in a safe environment what they see, hear and experience.

We have identified twelve sub-sections, which cover these areas. We have called them 'focus points'. They are set out in the diagram on page 21. Most of them subsume what might be considered the principles upon which policy discussions could be based. All are interlinked and overlapping. We invite readers to explore and modify the focus points in the light of their own knowledge, views, understanding and experiences.

These twelve focus points provide the basis for twelve explorations and discussions, all of which follow this pattern:

i. introduction
ii. a case study based on observations of children and practitioners in settings

iii. questions for practitioners to consider and set against their own values and beliefs

iv. a section which contains theoretical discussions and arguments, called 'Support for Thinking',

v. a final section, 'Support for Practice', which outlines how the practitioner featured in the case study dealt with that particular representation of cultural violence

vi. our concluding comments, which put the section in context and relate it to the wider dimension of the book

Real teaching and learning episodes and observations, and real images of children's play and experiences, are used throughout, and reference is made to relevant policies and legislation. At times the authors found it particularly helpful to weave theoretical discussions into actual practice in order to identify what children are really doing and then to focus on the more immediate responses of the adult. References to the background literature are used to confirm or challenge assumptions and practice, and so prompt further examination of the issues. Reflection, sensitivity and in-depth discussion are crucial ways to support and develop pedagogical practice.

Finally, the authors need to make it clear where they are themselves coming from. It is well known that for busy practitioners working in settings and handling daily the needs and demands of children and their families, the time and opportunity to discuss issues in depth with colleagues is a luxury. Despite this, practitioners are required to be well informed so that they can respond sensitively, confidently and immediately to the range of ideas and behaviours exhibited by children.

The importance of pondering, challenging, hypothesising and examining beliefs and values is overtaken by the need to respond to the immediate. However, the authors firmly believe that discussions with other professionals and parents, together with critical analytical thinking, are essential to the process of developing our approach to children, and that unpacking and examining values, beliefs, concerns and questions is a vital part of good practice (Day 1999; Moyles et al. 2002).

Individuals and settings must find time for these things, however difficult this might seem. It is hoped that, through engaging in a reflective journey through this book, readers will be supported in their thinking and will be able to review and re-determine what they believe to be the appropriate ways to support children, parents and other adults in their settings.

Twelve Underpinning Focus Points

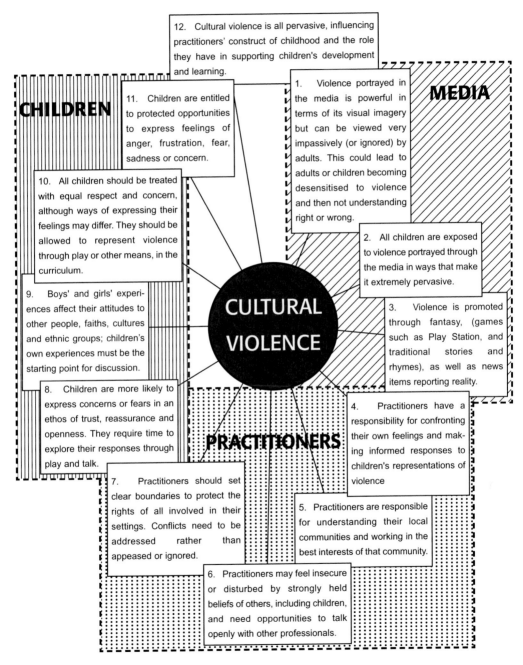

12. Cultural violence is all pervasive, influencing practitioners' construct of childhood and the role they have in supporting children's development and learning.

CHILDREN

11. Children are entitled to protected opportunities to express feelings of anger, frustration, fear, sadness or concern.

10. All children should be treated with equal respect and concern, although ways of expressing their feelings may differ. They should be allowed to represent violence through play or other means, in the curriculum.

9. Boys' and girls' experiences affect their attitudes to other people, faiths, cultures and ethnic groups; children's own experiences must be the starting point for discussion.

8. Children are more likely to express concerns or fears in an ethos of trust, reassurance and openness. They require time to explore their responses through play and talk.

MEDIA

1. Violence portrayed in the media is powerful in terms of its visual imagery but can be viewed very impassively (or ignored) by adults. This could lead to adults or children becoming desensitised to violence and then not understanding right or wrong.

2. All children are exposed to violence portrayed through the media in ways that make it extremely pervasive.

3. Violence is promoted through fantasy, (games such as Play Station, and traditional stories and rhymes), as well as news items reporting reality.

CULTURAL VIOLENCE

PRACTITIONERS

4. Practitioners have a responsibility for confronting their own feelings and making informed responses to children's representations of violence

5. Practitioners are responsible for understanding their local communities and working in the best interests of that community.

7. Practitioners should set clear boundaries to protect the rights of all involved in their settings. Conflicts need to be addressed rather than appeased or ignored.

6. Practitioners may feel insecure or disturbed by strongly held beliefs of others, including children, and need opportunities to talk openly with other professionals.

PART ONE

A culture of violence? Principles and practice

THE MEDIA AND CULTURAL VIOLENCE
The ways in which violence and terrorism are now communicated to young children

Focus One

1

Violence portrayed in the media is powerful in terms of its visual imagery but can be viewed very impassively (or ignored) by adults. This could lead to adults or children (or both) becoming desensitised to violence, with the possible consequence of losing their ability to understand the difference between right or wrong.

Introduction

Violent images abound in the mass media. In covering the news, press and television programmes are, of course, reporting a violent world. However, it could be argued that there is a lack of balance in the representation of violent and non-violent events; a shooting is likely to receive major attention, whereas a selfless act of kindness is less likely to make the headlines. Violence also pervades much of the material offered as entertainment.

Television programmes aimed at both children and adults often contain scenes of violence. Violence is paraded as normal – even acceptable – behaviour in many 'soaps', drama series, films, cartoons and other forms of popular entertainment. Delivered through the same screen, children also frequently see violent images associated with real life. For example, advances in satellite communications have allowed news reporters into the very heart of situations of violence and conflict. Competition within and between various media leads each report to try for the most shocking and dramatic images. Potentially this could make it difficult for children to separate reality from fantasy. This is especially likely when media coverage of, for example, a soldier in a hostage situation, might include substantial personal detail about those involved. In the child's eyes that soldier becomes someone's mummy or daddy. This makes the news items more relevant and more accessible to the young child, but also more threatening. Whether the medium is television, video, radio or magazines, children must be supported by sensitive and informed intervention from adults so that they can put emotionally charged situations and events into perspective. This will ensure that they are not ignored or viewed as everyday, matter-of-fact events.

Case study

The practitioner, Claire, has noticed that Jack and Harry are playing in the dressing-up area. They are using Red Riding Hood's cape to represent their own combination of Spiderman and Superman. Claire has noticed that their play is becoming boisterous and that the two boys frequently dominate this area. Their verbal and body language becomes increasingly more aggressive with the result that on this occasion the three other players, Sadie, Jane and Isaac, leave the area.

Claire is unsure what has prompted this level of aggression in their play. She has noticed a recurring theme of Spiderman and Superman images in the children's birthday cards and books from home, and so is aware of the boys' interest in these super-heroes. Claire is concerned that the play always 'brings out the worst' in the boys and is uncertain whether banning such play will address the problem or simply make it worse.

Questions for practitioners

1. In your experience, how do powerful images such as those affecting Jack and Harry influence children's play?

2. Why does it seem that children, especially boys, like to emulate superheroes? Is it your experience that superhero play appears to 'bring out the worst in the boys'?

3. Do children appear to understand degrees of violence, or is it all just a game?

4. Is it possible that, without justification, adults attribute levels of violence to children's natural and innocent exploratory play? Or is it that from a very young age children are being desensitised to aggressive behaviour?

5. What is your own response to superheroes?

6. To what extent are young children able to understand the difference between reality and fiction, right and wrong, good and bad?

7. How far have you discussed your own views with your colleagues?

8. How do the adults in your setting react to violent play? Do they challenge it? ignore it? or just passively accept it?

9. How far do you feel that all of us, adults as well as children, have become desensitised to violent images on television?

Supporting thinking

Let us consider for a moment some of the media images which have been created to appeal to children and have proved very popular.

Although not related directly to terrorism, the image of Spiderman illustrates how powerful media-generated superheroes have become. Young children are avid consumers of these. Their interest usually begins with an interest in benign characters such as Bob the Builder, Nemo, Buzz Lightyear and similar cartoon characters designed to attract very young children. Sometimes there is a violent dimension to these, which children find exciting: Bruce, the shark in 'Finding Nemo'; The Evil Zorg in 'Toy Story 2'. Children move almost imperceptibly through different approaches to and levels of violence. The transition from an innocent 'Bob' to 'Monsters Inc.', with its confusion of heroes, its bizarre monsters and its scream-making machines, to the more adventurous Spiderman, and then to more aggressive heroes, is so gradual it is hardly noticeable. Linking the more violent consumer-driven characters to the educational curriculum, or associating them with products such as birthday cards, clothing and toys renders them more attractive and desirable to children. Their all-pervasiveness increases their accessibility and makes it harder for parents to protect their children from exposure to them. Many practitioners will naturally seek to capitalise on those things which appear to interest, engage and motivate young children, but many also question whether promoting such superheroes is a good idea.

Simple factors which characterise many of the more violent images are the use of colour and shape. This is done so subtly that few are aware of it, though most absorb the effects. For example, consider the image of Spiderman. The impression of strength and power is conveyed through the depth of colour – deep reds and vibrant blues. The figure is often depicted crouching, as if to spring, which conveys impressions of action and power. Superheroes are often masked. The whole concept of the face being concealed, with 'steely', expressionless eyes peering through slits gives its own messages, too.

Images of Violence

It has been found that, even where these characters have been banned in play settings, children (especially boys) still continue to construct weapons and involve superheroes in their dramatic play (Holland 1999; 2003). Kenway and Bullen (2001) suggest that concepts of children and childhood have been influenced by a consumer-media culture, in which young children are developed as consumers and learn to relate to the personification of heroes. O'Regan (2000) argues that the media encourage children to be interested in aggression and violence at too young an age; Carlsson-Paige and Levin (1987; 1990) support this argument, suggesting that stereotyped good-versus-evil aggressive scripts impoverish children's imaginations and encourage aggressive behaviour. They acknowledge (ibid) the dilemma for early years practitioners: if such play is banned children will make toy guns out of Lego or similar, although they advocate that through informed adult intervention play might become more constructive, and less aggressive.

Holland (1999) also articulates the dilemma for practitioners in, on the one hand, trying to uphold a belief in the value of dramatic fantasy play as being 'central to the healthy development of children's representation and symbolic functioning' (ibid: 2), and on the other hand, not wishing to support the recreation of violent images. She concedes the necessity of children maintaining ownership of their play, whilst also valuing the importance of appropriate adult intervention in children's aggressive, war and superhero play. Smith (2004a) asserts that 'it is easy to feel uncomfortable when the activity becomes very prominent; and there is the possibility that for children who are already disturbed or who have violent tendencies, sanctioning violent play can make matters worse'.

He cites a study by Dunn and Hughes (2001) in which 40 four-year-old 'hard to manage' children and 40 'control' children were filmed playing with a friend, with no adults present. The former group ('hard-to-manage') played out more violent fantasies than the control group. However, in both groups the extent of violent play was related to poor language and play skills, and linked with other antisocial behaviours. Children who played most violently also demonstrated less empathy towards each other. Smith feels that the developmental issues regarding war play have still to be resolved.

After confronting her own uncertainties that the policy of zero tolerance of aggressive play was just not working, Holland (1999; 2003) conducted a series of observations in which children's sustained play was recorded (Dahlberg et al. 1999). Themes for the children's play included Power Rangers, Bat-mobiles, Apocalypse Wars and Robin Hood, although the extended play opportunities revealed no use of violent or aggressive language or behaviour. It should be noted that the emphasis in Holland's research is on boys' play. Toys offered by the consumer market for girls also promote stereotypes, this time of femininity ('My Little Pony', 'Tiny Tears', 'Barbie') but are not normally associated with aggressive behaviour. Indeed, one could argue that girls' toys 'dumb down' any chance the girls may have of playing out aggressions, frustrations, fears or assertive behaviours (Jacobson and Mazur 1995).

The work both of Holland and Carlsson-Paige and of Levin (1990) found that, where children's play was prompted by representations of media characters, children had difficulty in developing more inventive play, often being restricted to the limited actions suggested by the materials (Vygotsky 1978). Indeed, the teachers in Broadhead's study (2004) found that the more flexible the materials, the better the quality of children's play. It was only through physically joining in the play, being close enough to observe carefully and intervene in order to empower and develop the children's play that Holland was in a position to:

- model appropriate behaviours;
- challenge racist or helpless female stereotypes;
- model negotiation rather than resort to punishment;
- in the realms of fantasy, produce magic spells which appeased confrontation rather than causing violent death.

Images of Violence

In this way children were provided with opportunities to distinguish right from wrong (Kohlberg 1985). Not only this, they also benefitted from adult initiated opportunities to consider humane strategies for dealing with the conflicts they encountered in their play. Paley (1997) shows, through her stories about Reeny, a little girl with an astonishing sense of herself, ample evidence of challenging children's thinking and offering possibilities for extending or supporting their play in a subtle and non-directive way.

In our experience (Moyles and Adams 2002), many practitioners are reluctant to engage in children's play in this way. They feel that it is not quite 'adult' to do so, or simply that it makes them feel silly. Some practitioners have found that using a 'circle time' model to help the children explore ways of being assertive, whilst also being sensitive to each other's preferences for play in the classroom (Webster-Stratton 1999), has worked to resolve issues in a way that enables children to cope with some of these tensions. Others have found that it is vital to attend training on understanding gender issues to find out about the best ways to respond to and manage the very different needs of children (Askew and Ross 1988).

Supporting practice

Let us return to the case study which opened this section. After thinking about the issues carefully and talking with her colleagues, Claire decided to:

- speak with her head teacher about opportunities for further training to develop her understanding of gender needs. She is very aware that the level of aggression she observes in her group has recently escalated, and she wonders if this has been prompted by resources, by the boys' increased interest in superhero merchandise, or is simply to do with the current ages and stages of development of the children.

- try to improve her knowledge of contemporary childhood culture. She plans to watch some videos, read children's comics and view some of their favourite television programmes in order to understand more about the scenes, characters and story lines the children in her class are introducing into their play. She plans to use this experience to select some of the 'better' features she finds, such as supporting each other when distressed or injured.

- plan for more time to observe and support children's play in ways that are constructive and positive. Circle time is providing her with opportunities to raise some of the related issues with the children, such as the use and effects of aggressive and threatening language.

- ensure that planning meetings with colleagues provide opportunities to explore the values and expectations of the significant other adults who work in the setting. She will probably do this by offering them her case study experience and asking for their views and actions.

Claire, like all adults working with young children, has found she needs to address violence expressed through the media in a balanced way that doesn't over-emphasise its effects, but certainly does not ignore them.

Focus Two

2

All children are exposed to violence portrayed in the media; the effects of this can emerge in unexpected and unpredictable ways that may alarm or shock adults.

Introduction

Most of us have grown so used to a daily diet of media images that we become virtually immune to them. This is particularly true of television, which is an ever-present companion in many homes. It purveys a constantly changing stream of fact and fiction which forms a background to daily life. This leads to an uncritical acceptance of 'the box' and its existence.

As a society we have become so used to it that we can often be aware that the television is on, but unaware of what is on the television. However, sometimes there will come an event which is so cataclysmic, so visually and emotionally compelling, that it forces itself on our attention and we respond to it very differently from our normal viewing. Striking examples are the September 11th attacks, the BSE crisis, or the Asian Tsunami. Events such as these provoke a range of emotions, from horror, through outrage to distress and disbelief. As adults, we have learned how to cope with the way these reports affect our viewing, and with the diverse emotional responses they create: but what of children?

We all know from our own observation and experience that young children go through a spectrum of emotions and often express them in startling and extreme ways. Just think of the way a thwarted two-year old behaves! Or the uncontrollable giggling that might accompany a game. A complex range of processes, which includes physical, mental and emotional development as well as emulating adults, enables children to gradually learn to manage their emotions. Some parents and other adults are particularly good at helping children with this. The most experienced adults work from a basis of thorough knowledge of each individual child in their care, and they provide protected opportunities for children to explore and practise their different emotions through, for example, drama, role play and reading stories in which emotions are explored. Some children work through their feelings in unexpected ways. Consider 4-year-old Fiona in the case study below, and her response to September 11th.

Case study

Four year old Fiona makes double towers of large wooden blocks. Sue, the teacher, comes over to her and says, "It's nearly as tall as you are," and she shows her how to build up the blocks so that she can measure Fiona's height. The child watches while the teacher builds a single tower of bricks. When the teacher leaves to support the play of another child, Fiona reconstructs her double towers of bricks. She takes a play bus and fills it with play bus figures and then wheels it round the tower. She says "This is an alien car – this is for shooting at the people we don't like. The pilots are going to the seaside. Horrible people are at the seaside. They are going to be shot because we don't like them'".

Questions for practitioners

1. Would you have recognised what Fiona was doing?

2. How would you have reacted to seeing Fiona's 'twin towers'? Why would you react like that?

3. What, to you, would be the most appropriate way of dealing with Fiona's unexpected 'violent' response with the play bus? Why do you think this would be the best way?

4. Would you do anything to follow up this child's play representation? If so, what? And why?

5. What strategies would you use for enabling Fiona and children like her to explore their feelings about an event which has clearly made a strong impact?

6. Would you react differently if Fiona were a boy?

Images of Violence

Supporting thinking

Any glance at children's entertainment in a wide range of media – be it children's literature, television or toys – will provide evidence of the ways in which violent images are now barely noticeable because they occur with such frequency and so pervasively. As we have remarked before, the world is a violent place. It probably always has been. It's not so very long ago in the history of human kind that children would attend public executions. However, we would maintain that the violent images to which children are exposed to today have more potential impact because of their closeness, familiarity and repetition. After all, public executions were not repeated in news bulletins every hour, nor were they replayed in slow motion, the camera lingering on every convulsion and grimace. Images of violent acts, whether perpetrated by states, groups or individuals, have become an integral part of life – and therefore of childhood – in contemporary society.

The effect of the pervasiveness of violence is still not well understood, and is certainly under-researched when it comes to very young children (Lane 2000). As we have emphasised, adults and children alike risk becoming desensitised to the impact of such violent images. The more we, as early years practitioners, are aware of this the more we will be able to be sensitive to children's responses and reactions. Children are exposed to violence not only in material specifically created for them, but also in that which comes from outside the domain of children's entertainment. The 9pm watershed is an attempt by broadcasters to shield children from unsuitable material, but there is plenty available before then. The news at lunchtime or around 6pm often contains scenes that shock adults. Recall, for example, some of the terrible images generated by the minutes before the twin towers collapsed, or the emotional and personal tragedies of those caught up in the Bali bombing. As an aside we might remark that there are also many young children who are not in bed by 9 o'clock. For them, and for the homes where a lot of the television seen is recorded, the concept of a watershed is irrelevant.

So far we have discussed the prevalence and impact of the reporting of violence on the news. However, it is not just news items that bring images of violence into children's lives. Programmes such as soap operas, which are transmitted before the watershed and are watched by children as well as adults, often feature extremes of domestic violence, where fights and verbal and physical aggression are commonplace. Similarly, radio coverage of news items is often graphic in its detail, with presenters relying on the power of the spoken word and sound effects to provide realism and drama. Images in newspapers, on advertising hoardings, in window displays, through computer games and some illustrations in magazines deliberately set out to shock and to affront our senses. We take these for granted and rarely consider their effects upon ourselves, never mind upon children (Commission on Children and Violence 1995).

In this case study it appears that Sue was not quite tuned into what Fiona was representing and this made it difficult for her to deal with the child's unexpected, 'violent' response. Had she taken the opportunity to observe Fiona's play thoroughly and to note where her interests and focus lay, she might have recognised that the girl was playing out issues to do with September 11th.

Sensitive, informed intervention can only occur if practitioners make time to observe children's play (Broadhead 2004). Heaslip (1994) recounts an episode in which a hard-pressed teacher raced into a child's play, mistaking a submarine for a tower and asking 'teacher-like' questions, such as 'How tall is it?' It is easy to see how a similar situation could have occurred in the case study earlier. Informed and sensitive observation might have suggested alternative ways of supporting and perhaps intervening in Fiona's play. Maybe this practitioner's previous experience did not lead her to think that Fiona's construction was anything other than a predictable, ubiquitous tower of bricks.

Observation needs to be active; a context in which practitioners' listen, support and accurately interpret children's actions and reactions (Gipps et al. 2000). From this active observation, long term planning - in this case focused perhaps on Fiona's spatial awareness as well as her reactions to challenging situations - can provide for growth in line with the child's needs. Practitioners also have to consider children's emerging social and emotional development (Webster-Stratton 1999), which is now informed by strong media messages indicating, in the case of Fiona, that 'If we don't like people, it's OK to shoot them'.

In discussing all the major theories of child development, Cohen (2001: 88) comments on issues to do with children's exposure to television and the media and their 'increased psychological sophistication to a much wider exposure to social interactions', particularly in relation to soaps and dramas. Parents and practitioners will agree that all children, but particularly girls, seem to be 'growing up' much earlier. The many implications of this increased sophistication should not be underestimated.

In order to promote children's social and emotional development, practitioners need to teach children how to:

- apply appropriate social conventions;
- operate within a group;
- explore their own emotions;
- be sensitive to the needs and feelings of others;
- build on trust and security in relationships. (Webster-Stratton 1999)

Practitioners will need their own training in how to interpret emotional behaviours presented by children. As well as making provision and time for observing children, practitioners need to enable children to explore and express emotions and develop strategies for dealing with intense feelings (Moyles and Adams 2001: 41; Ronen 2002). Perhaps equally, as our research showed (Moyles and Adams 2001), practitioners themselves need time to get to grips with their own emotions and reactions if they are going to be well equipped to support both boys and girls with their different but related needs (Watson 2004). It takes time to change attitudes. It also requires a preparedness to tackle some challenging issues!

Supporting practice

Sue, the practitioner, is aware of the dangers of over-reacting and bringing her own values and fears to the situation. Children often do build towers and knock them down. But she is equally aware that:

- the activity in itself was not potentially harmful – this type of play is part of childhood and very natural for children as they explore their own reactions to what they see and hear.

- she needs to question her own assumption that only boys engage in 'violent' play and that girls equally need the opportunity to explore their emotions and social relationships.

- children need opportunities to experiment with anger, frustration and so on. Sometimes this will be 'real' and sometimes part of experimenting with the emotions of others. Just think, for example, of how children portray school and the role of the adults!

- young children are still coming to terms with their own feelings and trying to understand their world and their place in it.

- arising from her observation, some children will need to be given greater opportunities to discuss their concerns following viewing of violent images.

- as an early years practitioner, she will need to learn more about how to interpret young children's behaviours, probably through greater opportunities for observation, and maybe further training.

- young children have not necessarily acquired, or been given, the tools with which to express their feelings, both positive and negative.

- children act and react in unexpected ways. For example, Fiona's purpose – to shoot the residents of her tower – was out of character. Because of this Sue decides to meet with Fiona's mother to try to understand this unusual behaviour.

- the family should also be involved so that values are shared. It is important to understand Fiona's family background, and for Fiona's family to understand that aggressive behaviour demonstrated in the setting will be addressed and discussed.

A particular point here is that, in collaboration with the parents and her professional colleagues, Sue will in future be able to plan for adult support within similar play activities and experiences, whether they occur in the setting or in the home.

Focus Three

3

Violence is promoted through fantasy in stories, rhymes and games, as well as through the reporting of real life events in the news.

Introduction

Many nations have a cultural heritage embedded in stories and rhymes, told by children and adults and passed on from one generation to the next. Many of these - rhymes, chants and jingles in particular - are learned in the playground. Often they contain larger-than-life characters, such as giants – Fe, Fi, Fo, Fum. They regularly show stereotypical behaviours. Princes are handsome, brave and dashing. Princesses are pretty, pink and passive. Many of these stories have violent themes. Everyone knows that giants eat little people (notice how careful Shrek's creators were to make it clear that he is an ogre, not a giant!) Or just think of the rhyme 'Three Blind Mice' for an example of how violent some simple and seemingly innocuous rhymes can be.

Since September 11th, Osama Bin Laden has been represented in the media as a kind of larger-than-life, 'bogie man', the sort of image often associated with fictitious characters and fantasy play. Mention of his name will promote different reactions in different hearers. Mostly these feelings are negative, but whether they are positive or negative, they will probably have no real and direct experience behind them. This creates a dislocation between the actual and the perceived which is hard enough for adults to handle, and even more difficult for young children whose grasp on the differences between reality and fantasy is less secure. Bin Laden has assumed the status of the shadowy menace, even more frightening because of his secrecy and mystery.

Racism also plays a part in the way many people perceive not only Bin Laden himself but also the international army of terrorists he is reputed to control. The vast majority of adults are adamant that racist taunts and jibes are unacceptable in a pluralist society. However, even children who

Images of Violence

have been taught that racism is wrong do not always realise that words which slip easily into rhymes and chants, picked up perhaps from adult conversation or older children's games, might be racist. Consider the example in the next case study.

> **Case study**
> Simon had been playing in a group in the play area. He came home and repeated to his mother, Ann, a rhyme he had learnt. He wanted to know the meaning of some of the words. Simon is from a dual heritage family. His mother is white and his father is black. Simon, 7-years old, had expressed some anxiety about the rhyme but was also being influenced by his peer group to join in the play. He seemed to want to check out that it was OK to repeat the rhyme. His mother could not bring herself to say the words out loud but confided to the teacher, Kate, by writing the rhyme on a piece of paper.
>
> 54321
> Bin Laden's on the run
> Catch the nigger
> Pull the trigger
> 54321
>
> The attitude taken by the school was to say that children of this age often repeat such rhymes and that 'they will get over it'. Ann was upset and shocked, and not at all happy with the response she had from the school in addressing the issues of racism and violence involved.

Questions for practitioners

1. What emotions does the playground chant quoted above arouse in you? Do you find it understandable? Innocent? Objectionable?

2. Are the same emotions shared by your immediate colleagues?

3. In your experience, have children's chants, jingles and games changed from those you knew when you were a child, or have seen since? Are they more violent?

4. On what basis do you reach this conclusion (observation, talking with children … etc.)?

5. What are the consequences of ignoring children's more hurtful/racist chants? What could you do about them? What are some of the consequences of trying to address the issues they raise with children and their families?

6. What is the difference between playing with words in an experimental and developmental way and using chants and jingles that might harm or offend others?

7. How would you respond to racist jingles or rhymes if you were to hear them in your playground?

Supporting thinking

It is important to be fully informed of national, regional and LEA requirements regarding anti-racist and equal opportunities policies in schools and settings, and what they imply for individual rights and responsibilities. These are always a useful starting point for understanding what is expected in any culture and community. Sometimes such policies are interpreted as meaning 'treat everyone the same', whereas in reality each situation will need to be reviewed in the light of what constitutes equality for all concerned. This is likely to be different for different individuals (Biggs and Edwards 1992). Equality, like inclusion, means ensuring that everyone has an equal chance to be included. But embedded inequalities in our society – and the fact that we don't all start from the same point – mean that individuals have to be treated differently to achieve any level of equality. Schools and settings are increasingly developing and implementing their own policies based on local needs, and this is a practice which we would wish to encourage. Development and implementation means not keeping policies in cupboards, but actively consulting, using and amending them as necessary!

The case study for Focus Two (see page 33) provides evidence of a practitioner who has perhaps not discriminated adequately within the changing nature of the child's play. The case study for this focus illustrates ways in which children's culture is influenced by the news and media through their peers. There is ample evidence that changes are occurring in children's play (Jones 2001; Klerfelt 2004). For example, the former 'bang, bang, you're dead' is being replaced by more graphic phrases, such as talking about 'grabbing someone's heart and pulling it out' (Katch 2001: 27).

Children's playground chants now include influences from and references to the wider political scene (Opie 1993). In this context we need to explore the ways in which media violence is accepted or promoted through fantasy and reality, in particular through the same media – even the same screen. Although there is evidence that children can discriminate between reality and fantasy (Costabile et al. 1991), there is also recent anecdotal evidence from a number of practitioners that there are occasions when children are not making that distinction. Simon's friends have altered the words of a familiar jingle to relate to more topical, and racist, issues and events. Is this just what children have done for years, or something more pervasive? How do we know?

Practitioners often find it difficult to explore their own responses to the impact of terrorism post-September 11th, and can feel very concerned as to whether they may inadvertently fuel a sensitive situation by their own potentially insensitive responses (see also the case study for Focus Four). In this case, Kate was also aware that her personal response to the jingle – she was deeply offended and disturbed by it – should not influence her professional responsibilities to the teaching and respectful care of children.

Similarly, as authors and observers we had to confront our own discomfort at the Bin Laden chant. We decided to refrain from censoring or sanitising the harsh reality of children's articulation of repeated rhymes, but that does not mean that we accept or condone them. What is right for the children, parents and co-workers in one setting may well be different from what is needed in another. Practitioners and their colleagues will need to decide together what policies and practices are appropriate for their own circumstances and environment. But what is common to all is the expectation that racism is unacceptable and will be dealt with by staff. The aim of this will be not only to support the person at whom racist remarks are directed, but the child who makes them as well (EYTARN 1995). A post-September 11th guidance document (DfES 2001: 2) stated:

> *Schools have a responsibility to ensure the curriculum addresses issues of difference and diversity in ways that counter any prejudicial assumptions made about ethnic, cultural and faith groups and their experiences and histories … [and] strongly partisan political stances [should be] avoided. False assumptions and stereotypes must be challenged with sound factual information.*

As well as carefull;y constructed policy documents which have been developed over a period of time, most schools and settings have worked to establish close relationships with their communities. This means that staff can be confident that a meeting with parents would be welcomed as an opportunity to explore children's learning, and in many cases this is preferable to recommending specific child-rearing practices (Katch 2001).

Many parents are only too prepared to discuss their experience of the difficulties of limiting their children's television viewing (Kenway and Bullen 2001). They realise that television can have huge educational benefits and that their children have access to more knowledge than previous generations. They also appreciate opportunities to talk these over with friends, the setting staff and other informed adults (Bagnall 2000).

Hampden Way Nursery School in Barnet developed an Equality of Opportunity Policy which provides some informative guidance which can serve as an example of good practice. A few selections from the policy are quoted below.

> *All staff are expected to respond to and report racist incidents … to know how to identify and challenge racial and cultural bias and stereotyping …*

> *We will work and live in harmony where differences are seen as assets and not disadvantages …*

> *We want children to: be proud of their own identity …*

> *We want parents to: feel confident to ask questions …*

> *We want staff to: support and encourage the development of each child's identity.*

In the section 'Aims and Values', the policy continues:

(Our aim is to …)

> *help every pupil develop a sense of personal and cultural identity that is positive and yet open to change, and that is receptive and respectful towards other identifies;*

> *develop the understanding and skills of all pupils to enable them to participate fully in Britain's multi-cultural society and make their contribution as global citizens …*

Many settings will have policies similar to this. If we fail to fulfil what we state in our policies then we risk condoning behaviour which has hurtful or racist elements. In considering the implications of policies on practice, Pearce (2003) urges that white teachers be aware not only of the needs black children and colleagues, but also the implications of their own whiteness and its effects on the ethos within their classrooms. For example, does the creative area provide children with choices and materials to enable them to represent their own skin colour? Does the home corner contain resources which represent a range of cultures, faiths and customs and which reflect not only the children in the setting but also wider society?

Supporting practice

Kate was unsure how to respond to this highly-charged incident and the emotions it provoked and this concerned her. She had heard the chanting herself, but had worried that if she took action she might risk blowing the matter up out of all proportion, 'making a mountain of a molehill'. She hoped that if she took no notice of it the children would soon move on to something else and the problem would disappear. When Simon's parents requested a meeting, Kate turned first to the school's equal opportunities policy. This declared that:

> *This school will not tolerate, and will respond immediately to, all incidents that give offence to others in response to ethnic origin, sex, disability, social background and age.*

Kate also:

- accepted that hoping the children would get over it and forget about the chant was not a responsible course of action to take. She realised that she had professional responsibilities to ensure that she promoted anti-racist attitudes within her class.

- discussed the incident with her head teacher. The head agreed that it would be a good idea to raise awareness of the issue by inviting parents and governors to a series of discussions on the impact of violent television programmes on children's play and language.

- drew on her long-established, open relationship with families in the school community and, despite feeling distressed and embarrassed, decided to share this incident with others in the school, including the governors.

• contacted the parents concerned, including the parents of the children who had been involved in the chanting. The behaviour was presented to the parents concerned as a shared problem to be solved, rather than as a disciplinary matter. Following this Ann, and Simon's father, agreed to meet the staff in order to identify potentially sensitive issues and ways in which they felt they might be handled.

• consulted a range of anti-racist publications, for example those available from www.earlyyearsequality.org.uk as well as other related web-sites.

By working together and considering all these aspects and ways of dealing with racial issues, perhaps using some of the many observations of practice as we have tried to do, staff were able to begin teasing out the particular challenges which faced their setting and to determine what action to take.

PART TWO

A culture of violence? From principles to practice

THE PRACTITIONER AND CULTURAL VIOLENCE
*Adult's reactions and responsibilities at personal
and professional levels*

Focus Four

4

Practitioners are responsible for confronting their own feelings and making informed responses to children's representations of violence.

Introduction

As we discussed in the introduction to this book, the events of September 11th 2001 have had a particular impact. There had been terrorist attacks before, but never anything like this. Subsequent terrorist acts – the bombings in Bali and Madrid, the countless examples of destruction from Palestine, Israel, Iraq – have created a climate where violence and atrocity is a regular part of the daily news. These activities have tended to polarise emotional responses to terrorism and violence. What one individual sees as an unspeakable atrocity is another's jihad; what one sees as a just war, another believes to be brutality and repression. Not everyone considered the attack on the twin towers a disaster, and the television images of celebrations in the streets in some parts of the world are a stark reminder of the divided world in which we live. Furthermore, violence and aggression are often seen as intrinsic elements of the male psyche. The media present innumerable models of male behaviour in which strength and violence are inextricable linked.

Many practitioners have felt very confused in their own thinking. In those circumstances it is difficult enough to articulate adult responses to the complex issues involved. It is even harder to consider events from the child's perspective. It is all too easy to think that the extremes of terrorism we see reported from other places won't happen here in England, but we have already dealt with atrocities in Manchester, London and other cities in the past and it would appear that the chances of further violent acts are ever present and potentially imminent. If we can't sort out our own responses, feelings and emotions, then dealing with those of parents and children (as well, perhaps, as those of our colleagues) becomes even more problematic.

Most children adopt the views and imitate the attitudes of those closest to them. This unsophisticated acceptance means that the responses they display in the setting are derived from behaviour learnt at home – from adults and older siblings in the home, and from the television viewing and print material favoured by their own families. These responses are inexperienced and it is sometimes difficult for the practitioner to deal with the challenges they present. But this we must do if we are to ensure that we nurture the whole child, understanding his or her individual perspectives as well as addressing collective needs. McNaughton (2000: 181) asserts, 'Early childhood education is highly resistant to pedagogical innovation because it rests on the ethics of individualism'. How we encourage individual responses while at the same time encouraging shared values is a constant tension for those who work with children. McNaughton goes on to suggest that we should 'move to an ethic of critical collectivism' if we are to see practice in relation to wider policies. In other words, this is not only an issue for the individual practitioner but something which is best approached through discussion with colleagues leading to the evolution of a common approach.

The next case study shows how one teacher was confronted with a post-September 11th issue, posed by the play of two children.

Case study Two children, Aisha and Harry, are setting out a town scene with wooden models, including houses, shops, a garage, cars and people. From a distance they look as if they are playing together collaboratively and amicably. They both appear deeply absorbed and focused. The village is carefully arranged and set out precisely. The children are talking as they play. The teacher, Richard, wonders whether they are playing together or are engaged in parallel play, so he moves closer to listen.
Aisha is setting up a domestic play scene, with the mother taking the children to the shops to buy various things,

---

looking in the windows and talking about what they see. Harry (standing beside her) is enacting a bomber ('the baddie') throwing bombs at a crowd of people standing by the bus stop. He then piles up the little wooden people on top of one another and brings a doctor and an ambulance to take them to the hospital. He stands the doctor on top of the pile of bodies to wait for the ambulance.

Neither child is impinging on the play of the other, or interrupting it. Aisha describes her play in very domestic, familiar and sequential terms. Harry talks in detail about the people at the bus stop and the man coming along with a bomb and throwing it at them. Richard asks Harry why he did that, and he says it is because they are 'baddies'. When asked what was going to happen to them next, Harry said he had piled them up to go to the hospital and that there is the doctor standing on top of them waiting for the ambulance. The bomber had apparently gone away.

Questions for practitioners

1. Like secondary smoking, how far do you feel that Aisha has been exposed to 'secondary violence'?

2. How do you feel about Harry's play? Are you ever in the position of suspecting that your own feelings are preventing you from understanding the children's perspectives?

3. Could/should you interact with children's play in order to alter or affect its nature or direction?

4. How do you decide when to intervene in children's play (or is it interference?) and why? Would the nature of violence or aggression in the play be a factor that would influence your decision?

5. How would you respond to children's anger – if expressed verbally or physically or even suppressed?

6. How far do you balance the needs of individual children against the collective needs of children within your class/setting?

Aisha and Harry set out their town

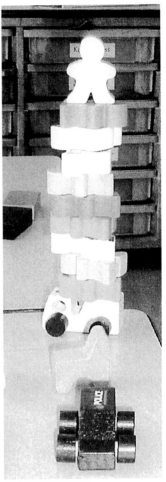

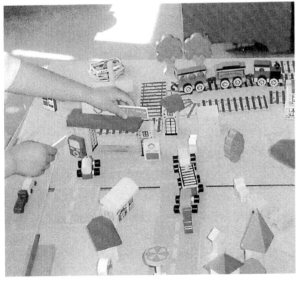

The bomber strikes!

The bodies are piled up with the doctor standing on top

Images of Violence

Support for thinking

The play in this case study is not unusual. Children, especially boys, often include 'baddies' of some kind in their play and most practitioners take little or no notice (Holland 2000). To a thinking practitioner, the play as witnessed in this case study would have been intriguing at many levels but mainly because of how the two children had set up the town scene together, placing shops, houses, the road and cars, vehicles, buildings and such like alongside each other. Yet while continuing side-by-side, they then embarked on their own completely different scenarios, neither appearing to intrude upon nor interrupt the other's stories. Both children were absorbed in what they were doing. Both were fascinating because of their quite serious intent. Although the boy was not actually playing violently he did make quite deliberate movements, talking the story through, and piling up the 'bodies' very deliberately and neatly with the 'doctor' standing on top of them.

Practitioners who encourage this kind of free-flow play (Bruce 1992) will usually see the importance of being ready to discuss emerging issues with the children. Talk enables children to organise their thoughts, and regular 'talk-time' activities will encourage the children to communicate with each other about their feelings, concerns and fears (Punamaki and Pijhakki 1997).

It is important to be able to broach sensitive subjects with children in the safety and security of your room, surrounded by listening and supportive adults. This will include helping children by offering appropriate vocabulary for them to use when they are trying to express their individual and collective feelings. It will include providing space, time and stimulating resources which will interest them in developing their play.

This practice of encouraging children to articulate their responses to societal issues is supported by James and Prout (1997: 4) who argue that:

> … *children must be seen as actively involved in the construction of their own social lives, the lives of those around them and of the societies in which*

they live. They can no longer be regarded as simply the passive subjects of structural determinants.

Richard, like many practitioners, understands that he is responsible for ensuring the acknowledgement of his own feelings about children's portrayals of violence, so that he can make informed decisions when facing such representations and helping each child to work through them. Richard has recently become aware of certain changes in the children's play and wonders if 'secondary' violence, i.e. that which has permeated the play from the media like an uninvited guest, is partly responsible for these changes. Discussions with colleagues are also invaluable. Insight into one's own reactions can also help practitioners to deal effectively with disturbing external events. Katch (2001: 5) suggests that: 'We learn to understand the children first by looking at our own feelings'.

Many practitioners will wish to empower children, both individually and collectively. However, in a professional capacity, most practitioners will have had to consider their own responses to September 11th in order to empower children and encourage their articulation of these wider issues, even though this sometimes contradicts personal ideals of childhood as happy, safe, protected and innocent (Kitzinger 1997). Richard respected Harry's entitlement not to answer questions about his play – but also arranged a quiet talk with him so that he knew how to discuss the implications of his play should he need to do so in the next few days (Farrell et al. 1999). Richard acknowledges that he finds this creates a dilemma. He believes that in some ways he has a responsibility to protect children from deviations from his perceptions of normal or acceptable standards of behaviour within society, rather than prepare and empower them to cope with the reality of the world outside school (Boyden 1997). Glauser (1997: 151) expresses concern for the 'street children' who are put at risk, or grow up without at least one parent and experience other forms of violence, e.g. domestic violence, within society. At times we will all be unsure of the boundaries of our professional role and will want to discuss these issues with colleagues (Day et al. 2000).

Images of Violence

Training to work with young children will prepare practitioners for thinking about children's gun and superhero play, but many will be unprepared for hearing young children talk about hand-grenades and introducing suicide into their play (Katch 2001: 2).

However much we've thought about it, the level of informed aggression in some children's play is disturbing and can offend many of our own personal values. Violence has always been a factor in the play of girls as well as boys, but practitioners report that the violent play of both genders seems now to be more extreme than hitherto. We have to consider how far this reflects our own limited understanding of the impact of conflict on children's development as a whole.

The violence children express can affect all our lives, and adults working within the early years need to learn how to address it. Help must be offered in a balanced way that neither over-emphasises nor ignores its effects. Some resolution of this may be available in exploration and discussion with colleagues both within and beyond the school, perhaps on a course at a local college or university (Erricker 1998).

Only by being informed in this way will practitioners be able to respond to children's experiences in order to ensure that:

- value is given to the well being, security and sense of self worth of all children (Mollie 2001).

- a secure environment is provided in which children can play and discuss their thoughts and actions.

- the source and motivation of children's play representations are understood by all staff.

- children understand that they are entitled to express and talk about their feelings and their awareness of things that concern them.

- children feel safe, supported and are confident their opinions are considered.

- our reactions enhance and enrich rather than inhibit the play of children.

- children are empowered, not ignored.

- children are not failed.

- staff understand the basis of their play representations.

- children can exercise their entitlement to express their feelings and their developing awareness of societal issues.

- children feel safe and their opinions are considered.

- adults act as guardians of children's emotional development and emotional states.

(See http://www.ag.uiuc.edu/~disaster/teacher/floodbib.html and numerous other linked web-sites for additional information and practical suggestions for working with young children.)

Supporting practice

Richard took the opportunity to observe, reflect upon and evaluate (Broadhead 2004) the ways in which he addresses his own concerns about violence. He also:

- made a brief reference during talk-time to Aisha's and Harry's play, offering Harry an opportunity to talk with the wider group of children.

- thought carefully about his own reactions to Aisha's and Harry's play.

- planned to discuss Harry's play and his own feelings about it with colleagues at a staff meeting (Arnot et al. 1999).

- made a note to remind himself and his immediate colleagues that it may be as well to observe Harry's play expressions over the next few weeks and, if relevant, to discuss anything necessary with his parents; for example, is Harry becoming obsessed with the violent images he apparently sees outside the nursery?

- explored further evidence of the ways in which observing violence can influence children's development (Edleson 1999), in order to be more fully informed about the most appropriate ways to deal with Harry and children showing similar behaviours.

Images of Violence

As a thinking practitioner, Richard also spent much time in identifying other incidents involving different children he had witnessed (and ignored) over the previous few weeks. He resolved to be more alert to potential violent acts being played out by children. He is keeping a notebook to jot down the particular incidents, but also to record his own immediate and later reactions to what he observes. For example, how much domination of play by boys such as Harry is REALLY happening? Does this only happen when certain resources are made available?

Well managed and thoughtful discussions with colleagues help practitioners to share their concerns and ideas about the behaviour and welfare of the children in their groups. A properly structured discussion should allow everyone to participate, contributing thoughts and observations based on their own experiences.

Focus Five

5

Practitioners are responsible for understanding their local communities and working in the best interests of that community.

Introduction

In the last section we discussed divergent views of some acts of violence and terror. We also noted that children absorb and adopt the views expressed in their own families and communities. There are also, of course, children who have a direct and terrible experience of violence in their own lives.

Within all communities there will be a broad range of faiths, backgrounds, cultures, ethnic groups and individuals, all holding different views, beliefs and reactions to political events or events such as September 11th. Equally, the children within that community will be influenced by what they hear, see and experience, and will inevitably bring those values into the setting. This is part of the 'whole child' (and children as a whole!) about which we are all concerned. Practitioners have to adapt and adjust their own thinking and practices in order to accommodate the full range of the community, dealing with children both as individuals and as a group of people who are growing and developing.

Sadly, some children may have arrived in this country from war zones. Others may have experienced significant financial, political and cultural hardship. Yet others may be refugees or asylum seekers from a wide range of linguistic, faith and cultural backgrounds (Hyder 2004). All of these children will have specific needs that will challenge even the most knowledgeable professionals within the Foundation Stage. Practitioners have a responsibility to find out as much as they can about the communities in which they work so that they can provide informed support for children, families and the wider locality (Moyles et al. 2001). The following story illustrates this need.

Case study   Maureen, the deputy headteacher, is a highly experienced teacher who has given much thought to violence in children's play. In particular she has initiated discussions with staff regarding the use of guns in play. She has been talking with colleagues about Rami and about the issue of guns and weapons. Maureen has explained that Rami is, to her, a very disaffected and aggressive child, yet only 3.5 years old. He has seen extreme violence in his country of origin before starting nursery in Maureen's school. She explains that Rami's family were open with her. She knows of some terrible things that happened to them and she understands the child's needs to express his inner thoughts, emotions and feelings. At first she was inhibited by not knowing how to communicate with Rami in his mother tongue. His play always involves soldiers, and often results in him hitting other children or toys on the head. Other staff have been very disturbed by this behaviour and have instinctively wanted to ban weapons of any kind from play.

Questions for practitioners

1. Have you and colleagues discussed gun and weapon play in your setting?

2. What was the outcome? Why? Was your decision, for example, related to known facts about children and weapon play? Or to your own feelings?

3. Do you have a policy about weapon play in your setting?

4. How far are staff in your setting alert to children's representations of violence and why they occur?

5. How far are you aware of what children feel about gun and weapon play? How far do their feelings reflect the views of their families and community?

6. To what extent do you mentally position parents as 'other' to yourself? (McNaughton 2000: 206)

7. How far do you discuss the violence which the children may see and experience or represent in their play?

8. How well does your curriculum reflect the diversity of perspectives, world views, experiences, values and traditions present in today's society and in your local community?

Supporting thinking

Several things are clear from Rami's behaviour. As Morley-Williams et al. (1995: 48) point out:

> The internal working model of relationships reflects earlier experiences. The quality of these influences children's sense of self and also expectation of how they can form relationships with others.

Rami's previous experiences meant that he was able to understand only violent human interactions, where people shoot each other rather than talk. He is unable to imagine any other way of behaving, or to share a sense of humour, be open and communicative or, at present, seek out new experiences (Sayeed and Guerin 2000). It will probably take much time before he is able to do this, but playing out his experiences with informed and sensitive adults will be vital to his overcoming this stage and moving into more flexible and creative play (ibid: 33; Alibhai 1987). Staff in settings need to address the issues by considering their own approach to gun and weapon play and ensuring that they have given the whole issue deep consideration based on their collective knowledge of children and their social, emotional, physical and cognitive development. An understanding, particularly of emotional development, is vital if each child's needs are to be handled appropriately (Erricker 1998).

Holland (2000) provides details of the processes of consideration she employed in examining her policy towards gun play. She explains that even when children were discouraged or forbidden from using guns, many children would continue with covert gun play or even 'lie creatively about what they had made, e.g. "It's not a gun - it's a hair-dryer".' (ibid: 92). Intuitive responses of personal confrontation or anger were not uncommon when staff observed children wielding guns or other 'threatening' toys. Consequently it was important that staff took opportunities to explore and discuss personal responses to the use of guns and similar resources in children's play (Broadhead 1992), both among themselves and with the wider community.

Holland (2000) concludes that in focusing on the content of children's play and on their behaviour rather than on the toys children were using, it was found that it was not possible to confirm the causal link between guns and aggressive behaviour. Orpinas et al. (1999) suggest that additional factors, including parental relationships and low levels of parental support, can also be indicative of children's expressions of aggressive behaviour.

Goldstein and his colleagues (1994) found little evidence in a range of research reported that the use of guns promoted children to act and think aggressively. In fact those children who, over time, were allowed to use guns and other weapons, soon tired or grew out of such play, whilst those who were 'banned' continued surreptitiously to play with 'guns' in whatever guise (Connor 1989).

Let us return to the story in the case study. It appears that discouraging Rami from using guns in his play may provide opportunities for him to articulate his experiences, instead of trying to work through them by playing out the violence he has witnessed and displaying aggressive behaviour (Ablon 1996). The intention is not to minimise the issue of aggression. Concern is raised by Kenway and Bullen (2001) about the degree of violence promoted through the media, and particularly about that which is aimed mainly at boys, in which superiority and power are linked with strength and violent action. The intention is to bring the aggression and the reasons for its occurrence out into the open so that it can be observed, interpreted and dealt with in an informed and beneficial way. Moyles and Musgrove (2003: 27) suggest that adults can model effective problem solving approaches in play activities through, for example, thinking aloud.

Many concerns regarding things which happen in the local community can be conveyed through events such as displays or exhibitions – for example in libraries, schools, village halls – and supported by communicating through the networks of other professionals who are engaged in working for young children and their families. Suschitzky and Chapman (1998) give useful guidance on working with the community. They suggest that involving the community by inviting families and other adults into the setting openly provides rich opportunities for understanding children's backgrounds and, importantly, ensuring children know that their own milieu is valued. They also advise that the relationship between parents and professionals should be based on acknowledging that experiences and expertise are different but equivalent.

They state (ibid: 21) that

if there is an ethos ... of valuing all skills and experiences then this will provide a climate of equality. Children will then receive messages that their families and community are accepted on an equal level.

As children interact with the world around them, their relationships can protect or transform their identities (Gilligan 1988). McNaughton (2000: 28) points out that identity development in children is

a process in which the child actively constructs meaning through 'reading' and interpreting experiences, but is not free to construct any meanings or any identities she/he wants. The child can construct many and varied meanings but they are limited to the alternatives made available to them ... [children] form identities in a highly controlled marketplace.

McNaughton (ibid: 28/9) suggests that

the challenge in early childhood is to counter those images of identity formation that have underdeveloped' or have resulted from 'simplistic understandings' of the relationship between the child and his/her family and community. The strong messages are that we cannot and must not underestimate the role of the family and community in children's development and behaviours.

Supporting practice

Partly because of Rami's experiences and his representations of violence in his play, Maureen believes that the nursery and the school should consider changing its policies on gun play. Previously gun play has been banned. Instead of our usual list, in this case we allow Maureen to explain in her own words what happened in and around a series of staff meetings.

We had a big debate about whether to allow gun play. Many staff were really against it and were concerned that they over-interpret what they thought the children should feel, especially as after September 11th all the children and families of all cultures in our community came into school, saying how sad it all was. The staff understood they needed to be alert to the expressions children were showing and be there to meet their needs.

The staff decided to consider permitting gun play, but made rules to start with, such as:

- *children must only shoot in the air, not at others (this was eventually felt to be a very silly rule)*

- *children may only shoot in certain areas, e.g. big block area*

Eventually the policy developed into allowing gun play throughout but 'it must not interfere with work or others at play'. It took a good year to get staff to agree with this and some staff never really did approve. What we all knew was that there has always been gun play but children realised that staff didn't like it, so turned their guns into fire hoses or whatever.

But Rami made us realise that he really needed to represent in his play the violence he had experienced. He just couldn't stop shooting. He would fight with the children. There were just too many toys for him to choose from and he had no strategies or skills within him to deal with it all.

Maureen considers the issues herself before continuing her discussion with the children.

I often asked the children what it was that they were allowed to do in their play and they were very confident that they knew they are not really allowed gun play. All I used to say to them during that time (when gun play was not encouraged but they were playing it anyway) was 'I feel very sad when I see so-and-so being shot'.

Now, when something terrible happens in the news that is cruel, sad and serious we talk about it with the children. Children know the difference between news and films. Three and four year olds understand the difference between shooting and 'I'm only playing'. I ask a child 'How do you feel about this or that?' when I've noticed something that I feel equates with violent play. I talk with them about play that I think is 'questionable' at other times and ask, 'What is your game about? How does it make you feel?' It is so important for boys to be able to empathise and get into how others feel, which actually they're very bad at. Their play is really the gateway to talking about it. For children who have experienced violence, to tell them that they mustn't do it is shutting down the avenues for talking about it.

In the case study, all the staff and significant other adults ensured their practice is underpinned by the school's policies in order to determine ways to:

- enable every child to develop a sense of personal and cultural identity that is positive yet open to change, receptive and respectful towards others.

- support the development of the knowledge, understanding and skills of all pupils to enable them to participate fully in their own community and in Britain's multicultural society and to make their contributions as global citizens.

- provide an environment that embraces the diversity of cultures represented within local families and in the community (David 1994), including social class and family constitution.

- promote good race relations through the school or setting, e.g. challenge stereotypes through stories, or invite mothers and fathers to visit and talk about a typical day in their routines.

- help and support children in developing the skills they need to detect bias and challenge all occurrances of racial discrimination.

It is essential that practitioners plan for time to be involved in and to know their local communities. This should be followed by observing, considering, interpreting and understanding the thinking behind children's actions before intervening or offering support for their play. In the case of Rami, much work was needed with his family to counteract the effects of his racial and cultural background, his earlier life experiences, and the way they have provoked his continuing aggressive approach to other children and to play.

Focus Six

6

Practitioners may feel insecure or disturbed by strongly held beliefs of others, including children, and need opportunities to talk openly with other professionals.

Introduction

Many practitioners may be challenged by the actions and beliefs of children in their setting. This may occur, for example, if the children's views conflict with those of the practitioner. Or, as the case study below illustrates, in situations where the practitioner has not yet explored the issues and concepts represented in children's behaviour. Some practitioners may not be politically or culturally 'aware', so feel unprepared to make well-informed responses to children's play-ful behaviours, especially where children's play is influenced by such current affairs as the kind of global terrorism epitomised in the events of September 11th.

The processes through which practitioners confront their own values and beliefs may be supported best by opportunities to talk with people who have been trained to listen and counsel in non-judgmental ways. With this support the practitioner may be guided to explore personal thoughts, prejudices, 'hang-ups', or experiences before considering appropriate professional responses to the problems raised by children's play. Some practitioners may also benefit from the opportunity to express their own doubts, fears, uncertainties, anger, and frustration in a context of trust, in which professional standing, personal esteem and self-image are not compromised - even though they may be challenged.

Respecting children whilst not necessarily sharing their beliefs or the values represented in their community is a difficult path to tread. Resolving the problems it creates can demand high levels of maturity and integrity, which might be particularly demanding for the novice or younger practitioner. Even those more experienced staff, whose political and personal views are well established, may find it particularly challenging to sustain attitudes of tolerance, respect and understanding in circumstances where their own values are offended. All these issues need to be acknowledged and discussed openly in safe, trusting contexts.

Case study It is mid-September 2001. The children in the Reception class of a large multi-cultural primary school are working on a topic about their homes and where they live. Following much discussion, some children start to draw their houses.

Akbar lives in a block of flats (see the illustration on page 68). Pauline, the practitioner, is concerned that Akbar might be feeling threatened, having obviously seen many images of the Twin Towers and other damaged buildings in the news.

Akbar continued with his drawing, and included a number of different sized aeroplanes – about 5-6 in various colours. He also drew buildings that they are crashing into. He described the picture: 'It's the bad people in the aeroplanes'.

Initially, Pauline isn't sure if the bad people are the pilots, the passengers or, indeed, the robots that also inhabit the picture. She realises that her own strongly held beliefs would affect her reaction to Akbar's picture. Unsure of an appropriate response at this time, Pauline says nothing.

Pauline is also aware that two children in her group were kept away in the aftermath of the destruction of the Twin Towers, in order to celebrate the 'success' of September 11th.

Akbar's picture.

Note the two robots on either side of the door. Are they to 'guard' the tower or are they the 'bad people'? This is not clear and the question was not asked.

Questions for practitioners

Whilst grappling with the range of emotions unearthed by the events surrounding the destruction of the Twin Towers, the following questions are worth exploring:

1. Should Pauline have commented on Akbar's play? What might she have said – to Akbar and to the other children?

2. How can the practitioner exercise sensitively the power she potentially holds over children of this age?

3. How can practitioners respect and support individual children when they disagree strongly with the values they see represented in the children's play, or those they know to be promoted at home? How do practitioners ensure they are making appropriate professional responses to children – irrespective of personal views?

4. How do practitioners ensure they are sufficiently informed and secure in their own beliefs?

5. Why is it so hard to make professional judgments on issues raised in children's play?

6. Why do there appear to be so many political undercurrents in children's play?

Supporting thinking

Many practitioners hold very strong opinions about issues of gun and weapon play. Others hold an ambivalent view, but will sometimes feel insecure, disturbed and uncertain when they encounter violent play. Opportunities to talk through issues openly among the adults who work together are vital (Carlsson-Paige and Levin 1990). When responding to questions such as those posed above, practitioners need to consider with their colleagues how to handle difficult events. This is a necessary part of the process of defining appropriate policy and practice. There will be similar dilemmas arising from the contrasting views and approaches of different cultures. These, too, will require careful thinking, informed by a sensitivity to the needs of the children, their families and communities, as well as reflecting the needs of the practitioners themselves (Wood 1998). Children's play will reflect the complexities of the world around them, as they learn to interact with others and to interpret the verbal and non-verbal behaviour of other children (Kantor et al. 1998).

In the case study, part of the difficulty facing Pauline is ensuring that children are helped to respect cultures different from their own (Siraj-Blatchford 1993). She was aware of the highly emotionally charged issues, relating to very deep beliefs, prompted by the events of September 11th. Nevertheless, she found herself unable to respond to Akbar's play, and so said nothing. Whether she should have said anything at all is a question we have already posed. We think she should. We owe it to children to have clear views about violence, whoever perpetrates it and wherever it occurs, and to apply them consistently. Practitioners must be very open, liberal, non-judgemental, welcoming and respecting of all cultures. They must separate their own views and values from their professional obligations if they are to support children and families effectively. However, acknowledging personal commitments to political issues can be very difficult. An effective practitioner recognises the importance of talking through issues in an atmosphere of safety and trust. Exploring uncertainties and attitudes towards the various different races and faiths represented in her class is critical to effective professional development.

Penny Holland (2003), in an expansion of her 1999 study, considers the issue of adults and power relationships with children to be a key feature in early years contexts in general. She acknowledges the need for practitioners to model carefully the use of power. As she asserts 'We have power and must use it wisely ... to use our power to colonize ... [children's] fantasy worlds is surely heading down the road of control and compliance in an altogether different direction' (Holland 2003: 100). Practitioners also need to reflect on where they themselves are coming from. McNaughton (2000) urges practitioners to think about how their own gender, race, class, ability and sexuality influence their practices. For example, what is your definition of masculinity? And is it necessary to redefine, in the context of your setting, what it means to be 'strong, courageous, likeable, admired by other boys/girls ...' (p.159)?

In addition to these personal and pedagogical considerations, practitioners need to be mindful also of children's curricular and developmental needs (Moyles and Adams 2001; QCA 2000). Much and Shweder (1978) suggest that children's language in day-to-day activities informs us of their cultural awareness and competence, as well as revealing their assimilation of society's morals and values. They also suggest (ibid) that, whilst the meaning of 'culture' is negotiable, it might include society's plans, recipes and rules for managing behaviours. Such cultural rules may be inherited - 'We've always done it like that' – or may relate to situations which promote such concerns as to whether something is legal or illegal, acceptable or not, right or wrong, true or false, useful or useless or, as in the case of gun play, permitted or not. Much and Shweder argue that 5–6 year old children are sensitive to society's conventions and their consequences, and that involving children in exploring issues raised during children's references to September 11th and similar acts of terrorism can help promote children's moral development. Later, the practitioner is led to ask 'What do I say with the children?', respecting that children have a voice to be heard and being mindful of the power relations issues.

The moral development of children begins with accepting rules as laid down in their families and communities, such as obeying simple requests. This awareness develops into understanding the need, for example, to keep a promise or not to lie, before developing into more sophisticated reflections about the interests of other people (Wilson 1985: 230). As Holland indicates (2003: 100): 'If … we use our power sparingly and reflectively, might we not teach children that it is possible to negotiate across difference and that force against force is not the only response to conflict?' Webster-Stratton (1999) suggests that developing proactive strategies to difficult situations can help create a constructive and supportive atmosphere within a class setting. For instance, articulating a set of professional values – such as ignoring or re-directing children's behaviour - can help in resolving pedagogical episodes (ibid). Talking about practice and asking difficult questions about their own professional values can help practitioners become more secure in their own beliefs (Milner 2003).

One of the moral difficulties for the early years practitioner is that children are presenting highly complex issues – beyond considering the interests of other people – which encompass the impact of behaviours on others and the place of rules, laws and government. These give rise to considerations which go beyond children's developmental levels or zones of proximal development, even though many of them may be cathartic for the individuals who feature them in their play experiences (Isaacs 1929).

Violence in today's world - in the media, in our neighborhoods and even in our schools – can make our children feel frightened, unsafe and insecure. Kids are hearing about and often must cope with tough issues at increasingly earlier ages, often before they are ready to understand all the aspects of complicated situations. Here are some things practitioners and parents can do to help.

- Create guidelines applicable to the developmental stage of children in their care.

- Recognise the implication that evil people exist who want to harm us. This adds another dimension to the task of communicating with young children, and the importance of making them aware of danger and violence without frightening them. Adults need to explore professional ways in which children's awareness of cultural violence can be supported.

- Think about how children will be affected by the repeated images they see on the screen. It may be unreasonable to propose that children should never see aspects of violence. It is suggested that adults make it possible for children to talk about what they see or hear, and discuss their concerns with them.

- Let it be known that it's acceptable to have feelings, fears and uncertainties. For example, they can acknowledge to children that it's all right to be sad, angry or scared, and that they sometimes feel like this themselves. Letting the children know you're human too brings its own rewards!

- Provide toys and materials that encourage play re-enactment of children's experiences and observations during a disaster can help them in integrating experiences. These might include fire and rescue trucks, ambulances, bulldozers, as well as building blocks.

- Ensure that there are plenty of opportunities to talk through issues openly, amongst the adults who work together, so that differences can be understood and, in time, resolved

Some useful web sites ...

http://www.thinkquest.org/library/site
http://www.ala.org/ala/alsc/alscresources/dealingwithtrag/dealing-tragedy.htm http://www.911childrensfund.org

All these were developed following September 11th. They provide further useful practical suggestions based on respecting children's development and, in some instances, their rights.

http://www.buildingbetterhealth.com/article/plainprimer/100234508 contains suggestions for parents on how to talk with children about violence

Practitioners should set clear boundaries to protect the rights of all individuals involved in their settings. Conflicts need to be addressed rather than appeased or ignored.

Introduction

The practitioner's role is highly complex and demanding - teacher, learner, enabler, guide, facilitator, listener, observer, parent substitute. This requires a wide range of skills. In addition, practitioners need to ensure that the ethos within the learning environment respects and protects the rights of all children and adults who are involved in their settings. This is one of the main issues in all the literature on equality – balancing rights with responsibilities and individual desires with collective needs.

It is inevitable that certain tensions will arise in trying to respect and uphold conflicting rights, opinions, experiences, cultural backgrounds or different responses to events such as September 11th – as illustrated in the case study below. It is equally important that these tensions are addressed and not allowed to simmer under the surface, which will only cause bad feeling and potential hostility. It is vital for children and parents, as well as for good working relationships within settings, that the atmosphere is conducive to trust, support and good humour.

> **Case study**   Jamil was writing. She was completing
> a story about Jack and the Beanstalk. The children had
> been asked to write about what it would be like when
> they reached the top of the beanstalk and where they
> would want to go.
>
> Jamil wrote that when she reached the top of the
> beanstalk she would go to America, where an aeroplane
> crashed into the tower. She wrote 'Hooray – all the
> Americans are dead!

Questions for practitioners

1. How far do you think that Jamil understands the words she has used?

2. What are the moral parameters of our professional role? What are the implications of being non-judgmental when the practitioner is confronted, for example, by two children who have been fighting? Are all children 'held to ransom'? Or should time be spent in unravelling the nature and cause of the conflict?

3. Is it appropriate to have set rules for children's play? What are the practical implications of setting 'clear boundaries' in children's play?

4. How can we confront difficult situations so that conflict can be dealt with objectively?

5. How do gender, class and race intersect in your life? How do they form / inform your identity? (McNaughton 2000)

Supporting thinking

Yasmin, a practitioner working in Jamil's class, knew from her recent training that she should assume children do know about violence (Webster-Stratton 1999). However, she was surprised at the strength of the feeling behind Jamil's comment and she was was unsure how she should respond. Nothing she had encountered before had prepared her quite for this. She now, however, understood Katch's declaration (2001: ix):

> *'It takes courage for a teacher to allow children to play out the latest scenarios racing around in their heads'.*

It is important that all practitioners commit to ensuring that their setting acknowledges diversity. Encouraging children to show respect for each other's cultures and religions should be a priority for the staff in all settings, including the room in the case study above. The staff also emphasise the basic need to care for each other and aim to ensure that children in their setting know they can feel safe and secure. In addition, it is also a place where conflicts are addressed rather than 'pushed under the carpet' and children and adults can express their views without being 'put down'. However, there are occasions when suddenly feelings of being threatened are introduced into children's play. In 2002, UNICEF proposed an optional protocol under the United Nations Convention for the Rights of the Child on the involvement of children in armed conflict, reflecting the increasing concern that society has for the safety and welfare of young children.

For details see http://www.unicef.org/crc/crc.htm.

Children are often exposed to violence at an early age (see the case study in Focus Five) and must be provided with opportunities within their setting to talk about what they see and hear in order to try to make sense of their experiences (Moyles 1989; Moyles and Adams 2001). Children need to be able to articulate what they observe, so that they do not consider further explorations of violent events to be either unacceptable or forbidden.

Practitioners also need to be aware of their responsibility to ensure that the adults who support them understand the values underpinning their practice. For example, in the case study above, it is clear that children are encouraged to be responsible for building positive relationships with each other (Martens and Meller 1990). Dunn (1998) suggests that young children will only have 'rudimentary understandings' of the emotions which cultural violence causes in adults. Their comprehension of global issues will naturally be limited by their stage of mental and emotional development, and will be based on their perception of more familiar contexts.

It is unlikely that children fully understand the consequences and implications of the exclamation 'Hooray – all the Americans are dead', nor are they likely to be aware of the nuances of social emotions, such as shame versus guilt, triumph versus defeat, esteem versus disrespect (ibid: 112). The complexity of emotions prompted by terrorist activities will be well beyond children's grasp. Therefore, in this case study the child would have been expressing sentiments about September 11th without possessing an informed understanding of global issues and their related implications. It was important that the practitioner realised this. Extending understanding of the local community and its history (see Focus Five) will help a practitioner to respond with sensitivity to the challenges of working within an area of changing and conflicting values (Nsamenang and Lamb 1998).

If inhibited by insecurity and uncertainty, practitioners will almost certainly decide to avoid direct discussion and ignore Jamil's comments (Webster-Stratton 1999). Considerations based on recent observations of children's play, however, may inform the practitioner's understanding of children's responses; for example, if children are currently attention seeking or physically dangerous to other children (ibid). A search through children's literature will reveal opportunities for presenting sensitive or disturbing experiences to children. These will enable the underpinning concepts to be explored in ways that are neither threatening nor hurtful. Haring (1997) includes images of disturbing events that children are invited to discuss; Kerr (2002) deals very comfortingly, but realistically, with the death of the favourite cat; McKee (1980) illustrates ways adults have of ignoring monsters; Nicholls and Cockcroft (2002) write about an owl chick who overcomes fear and learns to fly. Radunsky (2003) includes references to a boy who puts out a war by peeing on the soldiers. Root (2002) has written a life-affirming story with biblical references.

It is possible to support children's socio-dramatic play by ensuring the adult has opportunities to engage with children in the theme area of their room, or by providing resources that might encourage empathetic responses to situations such as fire fighting and medical emergencies (Grossman et al. 1997; Ladd 1981). McNaughton (2000: 44) feels that practitioners should divert children from violent play by removing home corner and block play and providing 'detailed alternative storylines and ideas for play'. Defining rules with children for their play also helps them to understand why certain parameters are desirable. The deeper responsibility for the practitioner is to provide an 'ethical approach' to discipline, in which children feel valued and respected despite any mistakes they may make (Webster-Stratton 1999: 177).

Supporting practice

Returning to the case study, after thinking about Jamil's unexpected response, Yasmin and her colleagues decided:

- that a key aspect of reflective thinking is to acknowledge uncertainties where they exist about sensitive areas, and bring them out into the open.

- that issues such as this should always be discussed with the senior manager as they are of great importance to everyone concerned with the setting and need a broader airing.

- to apply for LEA training, such as 'Working with Families within the Local Community', so as to learn more about other faiths and cultures and ways of handling similarities, differences and equality issues.

- to enquire about the Muslim and Sikh communities within the immediate catchment area, in order to gain understanding of the cultural, religious and linguistic backgrounds of the majority of the children. Extending understanding of the local community and its history will ensure that practitioners respond with sensitivity to the challenges of working within an area of changing and potentially conflicting values (Nsamenang and Lamb 1998).

- to discover how to access and utilize additional multicultural resources (Biggs and Edwards, 1992).

- through sharing experiences in their own setting, to develop strategies - such as knowing about and understanding different ethnic groups and their customs and traditions, both in the class and the wider community – which would ensure that the representation of different ethnic groups is genuine, respectful and appropriate, rather than tokenistic or stereotypical.

- to provide multicultural books and develop the home area and other role play contexts to reflect the traditions and cultures of the local community.

- to introduce into the curriculum opportunities to encourage children's sense of responsibility towards each other, such as activities in which children discuss how to be kind to a particular child in the class, or air the qualities about individuals that they particularly like and appreciate.

• to search the local library for stories that will direct children's attention and create discussion about the concerns and feelings of others, e.g. 'Angry Arthur' (Oram 1993).

PART THREE

A culture of violence? From principles to entitlement

THE CHILDREN AND CULTURAL VIOLENCE

Children's entitlement to be enabled to explore thorugh play and in a safe environment what they see, hear and experience.

Focus Eight

8

Children are more likely to express concerns or fears in an ethos of trust, reassurance and openness. They require time to explore their responses through play and talk.

Introduction

Part of the professional responsibility of practitioners is to provide resources and time that allow children to play through their fears. Children are more likely to express these fears and uncertainties in a secure and reassuring environment but there is no certainty that they will. As Baig (2002: 1) points out:

> [Children's] feelings and anxieties may remain concealed and, therefore, unacknowledged, or they may be expressed in ways that appear not to relate to their sources ... they may not know how to articulate these feelings or somehow feel it inappropriate to do so.

Research has shown that although a very happy atmosphere and caring attitudes are evident in, for example, some reception classes (see Adams et al. 2004), few practitioners offer sufficient time for children to play. It is vital that children have time and opportunity to explore, experiment and enact such events as they perceive them, and this is especially true of sensitive issues such as those brought to prominence by September 11th and other violent acts.

Case study   Marcus started the session in the dry sand, where he joined Chantal. They worked together to fill two large sieves that they had carefully attached to the side of the tray. Marcus was using a spoon to scoop and Chantal was using her hands. They made lots of eye contact, laughed and worked with increasing speed. When the sieve fell off, Marcus joined a group for construction, again with Chantal. Marcus worked carefully, selecting pieces to create a symmetrical model aeroplane. He smiled with satisfaction when he had finished and began to use it for imaginative play. "I'm flying really fast now!" he said, making aeroplane noises. Crashing into a brick tower he shouted, "Oh no!" He quickly built it back up saying, "It's your turn now!"

Marcus and Chantal repeated this 3 times, flying round, crashing into and then rebuilding the towers. Chantal looked increasingly uncomfortable with this level of aggression in Marcus's play and after a little while, unsure how to respond, withdrew from the play area.

Questions for practitioners

1. Is it possible to differentiate between play which is developmental and experimental, and play which is influenced by images of (and potential fears about) violence?

2. At what point does children's play become unacceptably aggressive?

3. What are the dangers of attributing adult values to children's play? How can we ensure that, while retaining consistent moral attitudes to violence and aggression, our adult values do not stifle children's opportunities for creative play?

4. How can adults ensure interventions and interactions in play are both appropriate and timely (see Kitson 1994)?

5. How can practitioners ensure they make interpretations of children's play that are appropriate, well informed and accurate?

6. What are the relationships between children's gender, class, race, ability and sexuality? How do these things influence children's experiences in the group and and their contributions to play?

Supporting thinking

In this case study the practitioner, Rachel, is conscious that the children in her setting often re-enact violent images in their play, sometimes as a result of witnessing violence within their own communities as well as in the media. From listening and talking with children, Rachel understands that many in her class also have experiences of observing violence through media (television and newspaper reports of war, terrorism and criminal violence, videos, DVDs, computer games) within their own homes.

O'Donnell et al. (2002) raises the concern that, because of children's physical and cognitive immaturity, they tend to respond to their experiences of violence within their own community with greater fear and confusion than adults. Practitioners need to plan for time to observe, consider, interpret and to understand the thinking behind children's actions before intervening in and supporting their play (see Focus Two). For example, in the case study above, it is only through observations that the practitioner becomes aware of the anxiety that Chantal is beginning to show (Gipps et al. 2000).

Whilst observing the children's responses, practitioners can consciously examine their own reactions to the aggression in children's play. Discussions with colleagues may confirm that a critical examination of personal views can be difficult. It is important that we listen to what children have to say. Listening requires a deep awareness and suspension of our judgements and prejudices, and is the basis for any learning relationship (Rinaldi 2001). It is important to listen to all children, not just to those who appear to have most to say. It is well known that boys are more demanding of adult attention. An environment in which positive behaviour is promoted and everyone feels valued and accepted is vital if all children are to have an opportunity to give voice to their ideas and be heard. Every child is entitled to an equal opportunity to access the curriculum provided (Suschitzky 1995; 1999; 2000) as part of the development of the concept and image of self.

It is important not to over-interpret children's play, or assume that any aggressive behaviour is always attributed to violence in society and the influence of violent images. For example, children's dominant approach may be related to gender inequalities that currently exist in a setting or community (Kenway and Bullen, 2001). A close look at children's actions and activities at lunch or play periods may reveal additional concerns regarding girls' and boys' behaviours. Boys generally will engage in games that are more adventurous and more physical than those played by girls. Boys' games are often competitive and aggressive. Girls' games often focus more on co-operation and personal interaction. Boys' games are more likely to 'evolve into rough-and-tumble and perhaps even simulated or real violence' (Brown 1994: 60).

It is unwise to assume that any gender differences are automatically related to possible cultural inequalities (Schwartz et al. 2003). In the case study above, the practitioners' reflections on the complexity of early years pedagogy demand that additional studies are made in the setting of equal opportunities for boys and girls (Moyles and Adams 2001). Practitioners may wish to ask themselves, 'What is it that we want boys and girls to learn from e.g. block play or the home corner?' (McNaughton 2000: 13), although it was found in the StEPs research that teachers often find it difficult to respond to even basic questions about their practice (Moyles and Adams 2001). It seems that we rarely manage to find the time or opportunity to stop long enough to ask these types of questions. However, they are vital if we are to address gender inequalities and differences, be open-minded about children's play and talk, and be in a position of knowledge to offer appropriate amounts of time to more critical questioning of practice.

McNaughton (2000) goes on to suggest that practitioners will not be able to change gender specific behaviours without a lot of effort and thought! However, it is possible to ensure, for example, that boys and girls have different play opportunities for differing periods of time and with a range of resources that might reflect their preferences, such as footballs, marbles and skipping ropes (Brown 2001:52). To this we must add that it is essential for each gender to have opportunities to and experience of the types of play usually favoured by the other.

In this case study the practitioner's immediate concerns must be based on helping Marcus understand that his over-enthusiastic play appears to have resulted in other children feeling threatened. Children should also be helped to understand that aggressive play can affect the time and opportunity that others might have for play.

Supporting practice

Rachel used this episode to reflect critically on her practice and took several different approaches to considering the issues it raised. She:

- set up a meeting with the other early years staff to ensure they have adequate opportunities to evaluate their practice, particularly in relation to gender related play.

- began to address the gender related aspects of her approach and the time given to both boys and girls for play.

- explored other influences on the children's behaviour, within the setting and outside it.

- discussed the issues with the head teacher, who suggested that the staff should examine the school's recently updated equal opportunities and anti-racist policy to ensure that it is integral to all children's learning experiences, and not just applied in response to emerging (or emergency!) needs.

- ensured that children's developing concepts of justice and equality were not distorted by a lack of thoroughness in her own practice, so that she continually made a point of discussing with children the qualities of different individuals.

- used professional judgement and insight gained through observing and talking with the children to share her interpretations of children's play. For instance, in the case study above, the early years staff concluded that Marcus's constructional play - crashing a model aeroplane into a brick tower - is little more than over-energetic behaviour.

It is essential that practitioners plan for time to observe, consider, interpret and understand the thinking behind children's actions before intervening in their play. Play must be planned for in the same way as other areas of the curriculum (Moyles 1994). Evaluations of playful activities in the classroom must be informed by observation. In the case study above, it was considered that the boys were beginning to dominate certain resource areas, especially during periods of free choice. Because of this, plans were made to introduce different resources that would be attractive to boys - such as a sports and leisure shop, a chef's kitchen, and a toolshop.

Focus Nine

9

Boys' and girls' experiences affect their attitudes to other people, faiths, cultures and ethnic groups: children's own experiences must be the starting point for discussion.

Introduction

Practitioners are familiar with the many issues and concerns about the different ways in which boys and girls behave. An obvious example is the way in which children of both genders respond to images of violence and terrorism. Some practitioners consider that 'boys will be boys' (McNaughton 2000: 11) and that young males have been obsessed with gun and weapon play for a long time. In other words, what we are seeing now is part of the male psyche and has no particular connection with September 11th, or with Bali, Madrid, the invasion of Iraq, atrocities by the IRA or PLO, Israeli occupation of Palestine, bloodthirsty computer games - or any of the other depictions of violence to which children are exposed. In contrast, in many ways girls' responses to the same events are conspicuously low key; even, sometimes, non-existent. This prompts many questions about the different ways in which boys and girls, collectively and individually, react to the attitudes, cultures, and faiths that they encounter.

Case study
Andy has been playing in the block area. Niamh, the practitioner, had recently noticed Andy's play developing from 3-dimensional play to more complex structures, partly prompted by her introduction of a collection of new blocks, including T-blocks, curves and cylinders (Gura, 1992). Niamh observes Andy placing one narrow cylinder under his arm, accompanied by 'rapid-fire, machine-gun noises'. He aims his weapon at a group of children shouting 'gotcha'.

Images of Violence

Questions for practitioners

1. What are your experiences of (and reactions to) boys' and girls' stereotypical play?

2. What intentions might boys have when they make guns in their play?

3. Do you think girls are ignoring the violence which they see in the media? How may they be responding in less overt or obvious ways?

4. In what ways might the practitioner differentiate between provision she makes for the play of boys and the play of girls? (See also the case study for Focus Five.) Why?

5. How far would you go to encourage or discourage play that reflects the violence to which children are exposed?

6. In what ways is boys' behaviour being influenced by aggressive role models (as in the illustration below)?

Supporting thinking

In the case study the practitioner, Niamh, was enthusiastically committed to the provision of wooden blocks as an essential contribution to children's development (Gura 1992, and see the Supporting Thinking section in

Focus Eight, page 84). Consequently she planned for regular opportunities to encourage, observe and support children's play in the block area. The incident described in the case study was the first time that children had introduced guns into this particular area of the classroom. This sudden and unexpected development disturbed Niamh, who was forced to consider the complex issues relating to Andy's play as she determined how best to respond to his 'shooting'.

We have identified four key areas for Niamh to address:

1. Consideration of the existing policy and practice towards gun play.
2. The day's machine gun episode and its implications.
3. The support given for children's development, play and learning.
4. Supporting and challenging her own reflective and informed practice.

1. Consideration of the existing policy and practice towards gun play

It is important that practitioners are familiar with the current policies of their setting on gun play and related fighting behaviours. Practitioners should try wherever possible to engage children in the development of policies. For example, in the above case study the children had insisted that one rule should be 'no pointing guns at people'.

Children will respond to opportunities to discuss the different ways in which they might consider each other's feelings when engaging in types of gun or war play. Initially this discussion might refer to, for example, play in the home area or free playtimes, but it is essential that any 'class rules' apply to all areas of the classroom and that the policy underpins the entire curriculum. Children will need help and support in applying their own rules about gun play to new areas of the classroom. For instance, whilst aggressive gun play can occur with or without representational toys, children will need support in understanding that the act of being aggressive or unkind is sufficient to be hurtful. It is essential that the application of policies relating to equality and respect to practice should not be restricted to specific areas of the curriculum, but that all policies should inform all practice. Furthermore, it is important to acknowledge that adults, too, have feelings and emotions, and that these need to be recognised and taken into account. Webster-Stratton (1999:51) suggests that

> *The understandable impatience and frustration we feel towards negative bahaviour in the classroom undermines our ability to think strategically about how best to respond in order to modify the child's behaviour.*

She suggests adopting proactive steps towards supporting children's behaviour. Routines, consistent forms of behaviour and classroom rules help teachers to create 'safe and predictable' environments for children, both boys and girls, to learn and explore diverse aspects of the world around them.

2. The days' machine gun episode and its implications.

Observation provides practitioners with opportunities to interpret and understand children's play. Close examination of the context of children's actions, as in this case study, might help determine the focus of the child's 'attack'. There is a difference between randomly brandishing a make-believe gun - as many children, particularly boys, do - and specifically aiming a weapon with the intention of harming or upsetting another child. Observation would provide a practitioner with contextual evidence of what actually occurred, so avoiding a situation in which an adult over-reacted or attributed more sophisticated motives to what was really no more than an innocent act of childhood. If a child was clearly aiming a 'weapon' at a group of children, the adult would revisit earlier discussions with the class about the importance of respecting each other and not hurting each other.

Concepts such as respect can be difficult for some children to grasp. The basis of respect is empathy: behave towards others as you would wish them to behave towards you. Perhaps, as some maintain, empathy cannot be taught, but it can certainly be encouraged. Relating this notion to episodes within the classroom might help children to realise what is meant by the term 'respect' by putting themselves in the shoes of other children. There is one feeling associated with brandishing a toy machine gun. A very different feeling comes from looking down its barrel. Through realising the implications of violent play and the way that it affects others, children might be encouraged to explore alternative ways of responding to conflict; for example, 'playing diplomacy' by looking to discussion and negotiation to achieve goals, rather than always taking the aggressive route by 'playing war'.

It is important that children have opportunities to explore their own fears and anxieties, which perhaps have been fuelled by sensing anxieties at home for the personal safety of close relatives, especially in the aftermath of events such as September 11th. In the case study above, the practitioner reflected that it was possible that many children in her classroom were seeing frequent and detailed images of conflict, as at the time there was particularly intensive coverage of violent issues on news bulletins during the daytime and early evening when young children might be viewing or listening. Niamh knew that Andy came from a well-informed household, where there was interest in the news and current affairs. She realised that Andy was regularly exposed to images of global conflict, and it was likely that this had heightened his interest in war games. She considered that her priority was to support Andy's developmental needs through -

- continued observation and interpretation of his play.

- the provision of appropriate resources (including cylindrical blocks) to promote expression of his thoughts and concerns.

- exploring, informing and confronting her own attitudes towards current affairs – whilst also ensuring that her personal perceptions were not imposed on others.

Media reports of violent events provide many stereotypical images of male role models – possibly further encouraging boys' gun play.

3.   The support of children's play, development and learning.

Discussion with colleagues is an important aspect of reflective practice and can help promote understanding of cultural influences and differences within the community (Escobar-Ortloff and Ortloff 2003). It is often through engaging in conversations with colleagues, taking the opportunity to articulate concerns and understandings about children, that teachers begin to understand more about their own teaching practices (Husu 2003). In this case study the practitioner was aware of the dangers of promoting stereotypical views; for example, of passive Asian girls (Brah and Minhas 1988) or allowing the boys to monopolise her attention (Graddol and Swann 1989).

Children's experiences of and reactions to the world around them should always be the starting point for discussions between the practitioners in each setting. Children's experiences affect their attitudes to other people and to other faiths, cultures and ethnic groups. Because of this there is in such situtations the potential for the development of, for example, stereotyped or racist views. Niamh was concerned about Andy's intimidating behaviour and anxious to prevent any peer rejection or exclusion as a result of it. Through a series of whole class and small group discussions the class reconsidered their rules about guns. They extended their 'No Pointing Guns at Children' rule to include positive affirmation for friendly behaviours such as –

- sharing resources;
- suggesting alternative ways of playing together;
- asking permission to be included in play;
- asking for help (Webster-Stratton 1999),

Niamh was careful to ensure that both boys and girls contributed to the reasoning behind each role.

When reviewing or modelling behaviour it is often useful to be able to separate the actions under consideration from the conduct of actual children. Persona dolls and puppets offer useful vehicles for this. For example, through using puppets it is possible to model ways of listening and waiting to talk, taking turns in conversation, showing interest and inviting someone to play. Making socially acceptable behaviour explicit is likely to help children to develop the skills to articulate and negotiate their preferences in playful situations. Working and playing with boys and girls in a variety of locations within the setting – in the home area, the block area, outside and during free playtimes provides opportunities for practitioners to pattern appropriate behaviour whilst also observing and listening to their responses to different situations.

4. Supporting and challenging her own reflective and informed practice

It is important for practitioners to examine what they do in order to ensure that responses to issues are meaningful, inherent, and not – however inadvertently – tokenistic (Jones 2001). This is best achieved by developing a reflective approach and the regular analysis of practice, which will help to ensure that prejudiced attitudes do not inadvertently influence the many decisions which practitioners make in the course of a day (Taylor-Webb 2001). Revisiting from time to time examples of individual policies developed or adopted by a setting provides the opportunity to examine whether all practice is underpinned by the values and beliefs to which the institution subscribes. Following the events described in the case study, Niamh worked with other staff in her setting to establish a programme for examining the resources and literature they all used, with the purpose of achieving consistency of values throughout all areas of the curriculum. Regular review by professionals is essential. If it is also possible to involve parents and other significant adults within the community it will contribute to understanding the subtleties and complexities of different cultures and their sometimes conflicting attitudes towards gender (Arber 2003).

Niamh realised that boys and girls respond differently to violence and are likely to represent violence in very different ways. She was uncertain whether her provision was adequately meeting the needs of both genders. This is a natural concern, although we should bear in mind some caveats. For example, Brittan (1989) suggests that gender differences are highly complex and can change from situation to situation (Paley 1986).

Practitioners are often tentative and uncertain in what they do and the provision they make. This is not surprising, and nothing to be ashamed of! Supporting the conceptual development of children from a variety of backgrounds and environments is a complex and taxing task, and there are no easy answers. Being uncertain is associated with reflective practice and is essential to the questioning, questing approach which we are recommending as the best way to manage the issues we have been discussing in this book. In the context of this case study it is important to engage in a critical, thoughtful examination of the values and attitudes of all staff towards gender issues. This examination will take in a range of differences and similarities, and may involve asking challenging, probing questions about the values and assumptions which underpin practice (Milner 2003). Paley's work (1991) explores the classroom in which children discover themselves, the society in which they live and the ways in which they learn how to confront new challenges. Her approach helps children to make sense of the experiences they encounter both inside and outside the setting; she aims to help practitioners to make sense of and link together the complex concepts within the curriculum through listening to children and understanding their behaviours.

Supporting practice

This is a knotty area, and there are many issues to consider, which are best addressed through a variety of approaches. In general, practitioners should try:

- thoughtful listening and thorough consideration of the pedagogical issues related to gun play.

- extending continuing professional development through

    - researching the concepts underpinning children's play, including child development and deeper ethical and political issues;

    - considering children's developmental and curriculum needs.

- addressing stereotypical behaviours in children's play.

- referring to literature on children's play – including an excellent short book by Ross and Brown (1993), and in Moyles (1989, 1994; 2002).

- providing support to children in applying 'their' rules to their engagement in the curriculum.

- talking with colleagues about whether your setting encourages or discourages play that reflects violence.

- questioning the ways in which you may or may not challenge stereotypical behaviours in your setting.

- ensuring a wide range of resources that reflect the different needs of boys and girls is available for all activities and areas in the classroom. For example, in the dressing-up area, are boys and girls able to dress up as fire-fighters? or nurses? Are there clothes for mummies and daddies to work in the kitchen, take the baby shopping or go to work?

Much of what we, as practitioners, believe about gender has been formed through our own developmental years. However, this should not stop us challenging received views, whether our own or those of others, in a constructively critical way. No progress can be made without questioning why we hold the views we do and whether, in today's society, they are still valid.

Focus Ten

10

All children should be treated with equal respect and concern, although their ways of expressing their feelings may differ. They should be allowed to represent violence though play or other means in the curriculum.

Introduction

What does treating children with respect and concern mean? To what extent does it mean abandoning ones own opinions and values? Or at least relogating them to second place? Discussions with a large number of practitioners suggest a variety of views. What most agree is that respect and concern are dependent on many factors specific to the context and community. It is vital to understand these if cultural and racial understanding post-September 11th is to be promoted. Settings and communities vary, and there is no simple formula for addressing these matters. The approach will rely on the experience of the practitioner as well as on many factors specific to the particular situation. We hope that the section which follows will also offer some help.

The effectiveness of the practice illustrated in the following case study is based on the respect and concern for each child in her setting which underpins the practioner's approach to all the children in her care. She is able to build on the values and beliefs that were firmly established with the children as they were introduced to the routines of setting. Incidentally, this illustrates the enormous value of good indiction processes. In this case demonstrating respect in a dynamic community demanded informed skill and genuine sensitivities.

Practitioners' responses must be individualised and immediate – but responding with confident fluency will be dependent on a secure philosophy and understanding. In the case study that follows, a young Muslim boy prepares for his Eid Party. His prayerful play is totally accepted and respected by the practitioner and other children.

Case study

The Eid Party

In Pat's setting there are many Muslim children. She has been aware of Ramadan, and that the disciplines of fasting and prayer have been important in many of the families in the community.

Some of the children suggest that to celebrate the end of Ramadan they have an Eid party. Pat talks to all the children about Ramadan, and what Eid means to the Muslim families in the community.

During the introduction to the lesson, she discusses ways in which every child might contribute to the planning and celebrations of their party. The children suggest ways to make invitations and prepare food for the party – including 'cheese and potatoes'. Parents joined in the preparation, as adults and children donned their party clothes. Before joining the party, Mohammed confidently walks to the sink to do wazu, a Muslim ritual of washing and cleaning. Children nearby accept and respect his actions.

Mohammed performs wazu.

Other children watch and respect what he is doing.

Questions for practitioners

1. What does the practitioner, Pat, do to create in her room an ethos of respect for the individual?

2. How might practitioners ensure they have adequate knowledge and understanding of diverse cultures within their setting's local community?

3. In your experience, are there other events that may have a particular cultural resonance (e.g. other religious festivals)? How might you promote understanding and respect of these amongst the range of children in your setting?

4. The attitudes of some people to some races and religions, and to people in general with brown skin, has been affected by September 11th. For example, there have been reports in the press of 'Osama' being used as a taunt by racists against anyone with Asian colouring, and of Sikhs being abused and attacked. How might you respond to such attitudes if they were expressed by the children in your setting?

5. In what ways does being 'politically correct' promote or hinder effective early years practice?

Supporting thinking

The case study for this section and the stills on the previous page are from the video that accompanies the StEPs training pack for playful teaching with young children (Moyles and Adams 2001). A close examination of the discourse and activities in the video reveals various ways in which Pat shows respect and concern for all the children in her class.

This case study is different from the ones we have considered so far. It does not reflect 'violence' in the way that some of the others do, and so we propose to treat it rather differently. We have seen how children's attitudes and responses are often based on stereotypes picked up from the adult world. Knowledge and understanding are the best weapons against stereotyping. This case study shows us how one experienced practitioner exhibited her sensitivities to, and respect for, the children in her care and for the community from which they came, and how this enriched their appreciation of this particular religious festival, whatever their own background.

Some of the children in Pat's nursery decided that as it was nearly Eid they should have a party. Once she had explained to the children that they need to plan for the party, she invited contributions from some of the Muslim children. Then she talked with the children from Hindu and Christian faith backgrounds, acknowledging that they celebrate different festivals at different times and in different ways. Doing this encouraged the children to listen to and acknowledge the similarities as well as the differences in their individual faith backgrounds (Siraj-Blatchford 1993).

It is important that practitioners know about and understand the influences within children's cultural backgrounds (Giavrimis et al. 2003). In considering her own professional development, Pat ensured that she was well informed about the various faiths, traditions and festivals celebrated by the many cultures within the community served by her nursery. Children's images of themselves, each other and their role in each community, are informed by their cultural heritage. The internet offers a wealth of easily accessible, relevant and up-to-date information, which can be used to help develop professional knowledge and understanding of multicultural matters (DeWitt 2003).

The pedagogical episodes within the StEPs video were all genuine representations of current practice within each setting at that time (1998-2001). However, since September 11th it has been suggested that an 'aftermath of fear and sadness', and certainly concern, has been expressed by many practitioners, who are aware of the responsibilities they hold regarding children's responses to acts of terrorism (Kassem 2002: 363), particularly in multi-faith settings. Kassem (2002) argues that it is important to nurture the social and emotional competencies of practitioners, suggesting that currently there is more emphasis on practitioners' cognitive rather than on their affective abilities.

Ansari (2002: 22) acknowledges that 'Muslims living ... in Britain have had to think about themselves in relation to being rejected and constructed as 'other''. In the video, Pat displays evidence of sensitive and informed responses to children having a party. By applying the careful use of language, provision of resources and genuine respect for children, she ensures that she and her colleagues understand and value all faiths and cultures in various ways. Consequently they are all attributed similar respect and understanding and no child feels constructed as 'other' (De Witt 2003).

Pat is conscious that many adults today grew up at a time when there was little emphasis on the benefits of understanding the many cultures within society (Matthews 2003: 275). Matthews also suggests that children's rights to be heard and valued 'were not taken seriously' previously. Underpinned by a belief in children's entitlement to 'play experiences that are set in meaningful and relevant activities and contexts for learning', Pat ensures that the children's families and other significant adults within the community will develop an understanding of each others' faiths and cultures, together with an informed respect for the similar and different ways in which they express themselves (Moyles and Adams 2001: 26).

Images of Violence

In acknowledging their differences as well as their similarities, Pat aimed to promote and sustain within each child an awareness of her or his local community (Herr 1999). Through her concern for children's emotional development and their awareness of self, she embraced all cultures when celebrating various festivals throughout the year. This was helped by her knowledge of the various ethnic and faith groups in her community. Her intention was to promote levels of understanding, empathy, tolerance and respect amongst the children in her class.

De Witt (2002: 19) suggests that through 'critical pedagogy' the teacher reflects the local community in the classroom by, for example, representing different aspects of socio-economic and socio-cultural diversity – thus helping to promote respect between the children and their wider community. These diversities are evident in the video of Pat's classroom. For example, some children chose to eat certain party food with their fingers, while others requested cutlery. All children's preferences were accommodated. In case it was necessary, one child placed his mobile 'phone next to his space at the table!

Noorderhaven and Halman (2003: 67/8) suggest that a teacher's awareness of the important role education has 'in the transfer of cultural values ... [and] being educated in a multicultural environment, may conceivably lead to a better understanding and tolerance of other cultures'.

One aspect of Pat's reflective thinking about her practice was to consider the ways in which promoting understanding, respect and tolerance within her setting might influence the families of children in the setting. The video demonstrates how children may need to be treated differently because of their backgrounds, but that all should receive equal concern – as individuals and as a whole. Pat's philosophy ensures that, if children choose to represent violence through play or other means, they should be made aware of others' rights not to be subjected to hurt or distress. One child's entitlement to express himself or herself must be weighed against another child's right not to be oppressed or upset.

Supporting practice

In this video, the practitioner adopted a reflective approach to her practice, which was informed by her own experience. This led her to decide to:

- make a point of inviting contributions from Muslim children.

- ensure she involved Hindu and Christian children.

- accept contributions from every child so that all cultures and faiths were acknowledged and respected within the context of the Eid Party.

- demonstrate informed and sensitive responses to children.

Children are entitled to protected opportunities to express feelings of anger, frustration, fear, sadness or concern.

Introduction

Children will be sad if their cat dies and frustrated if their building blocks keep tumbling down. Is it possible - or desirable - to sanitise childhood so that they never experience difficulties like this or the emotions which they engender? If we aim to ensure they are always happy, do we also deny them opportunities to be challenged, to overcome adversity and to discover the satisfaction of achievement? Play is the means by which children explore and try to make sense of the world around them. In role play they will go shopping, take care of an injured baby, drive a bus or go on a picnic. They will also act out what they see on television, which may involve trying to process and come to terms with images of violence. We believe that children must be allowed to play and to represent violence in whatever ways are appropriate to them as individuals, as long as what they do is consistent with the rights of others not to be subjected to violence or physical or emotional hurt.

The case study which follows presents a technique that allows us to think about these issues in some depth. It is rather different from the others we have used in this book.

Case study   **The Helicopter Technique**

Not long after September 11th 2001, a child in a reception class told a story. This was a boy who had worked with us in the nursery class the previous year, and so knew the technique described well. Here is his story.

'Once upon a time there was a plane and he was going to crash into a building and make an explosion. And all

---

the people were hurt. And they got to die. And then the firemen came and then the firemen put out the fire.'

The story is chilling. During its acting-out the children were totally engaged. I felt unsure, out of my depth. Could we deal with this issue with five year olds? But I trusted the child. He wanted to play the plane. I was worried that we would be trivialising the issue, but I went with my gut feelings to let him set the tone for the acting-out.

Before we acted it, I asked how he wanted to show the building. He was very clear, and pointed to a place on the stage. That was where the building was. He didn't need it to be represented by a child. We started the acting-out.

The boy concentrated as the plane flew to the spot, and then gently curled up in a ball on the floor. I brought up five children to play the people. They very seriously took on their roles of being hurt, and when I read 'they got to die' they all lay down on the floor in total silence. The room was really hushed, all the teachers and children completely engaged in the action. Then I called up another five children as firemen. They stood up and walked among the bodies of their classmates, and very seriously held hoses to put out the fire. We all watched in stunned silence for a while. It was the closest storytelling/story acting has come to drawing tears from me. All of us, from the youngest to the oldest, were moved.

When we clapped 'thank you' and cleared the stage there was a moment of quiet reflection and then almost as one the children looked at me and said, 'Can we do it again?' I was surprised; I didn't know what to do, so I simply said, 'I'm curious to know why you are so keen to do that story again.' A girl sitting next to me looked up and said, 'Because it was really interesting.' So we did it again, because where I was confused, the child was right. She knew we had tapped into something really powerful, something that school and adults don't often let us tap into; a way of exploring our fears and the things that we don't understand, and of giving voice to the thoughts that we all have and that often we try to protect our children from discussing.'

This story is from Trisha Lee, Director of 'Make Believe Arts', who reports on a session in a London primary school during the winter term 2002. It is reported in 'Make Believe Arts News', Edition 3, January 2003. Contact: Trisha Lee, Make-Believe Arts, 27 Merton Mansions, Brook Mill Road, London SE8 4HS. 020 8692 8886, e-mail makebelievearts@aol.com

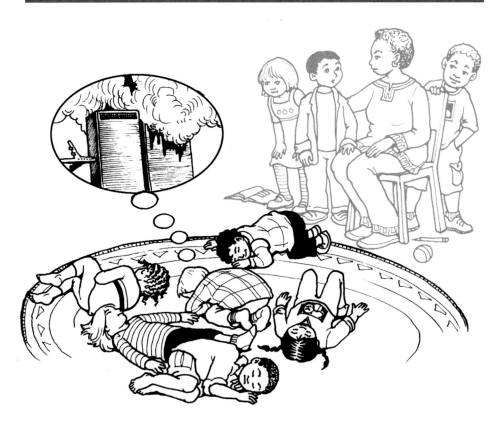

Questions for practitioners

- What do you understand is meant by 'protected opportunities'? Should we try to protect children from reality, including the reality of events like September 11th?

- In what ways might parents need to be involved in offering children opportunities to express feelings?

- What would you do if not all significant adults felt it appropriate for children to express anger or other behaviours sometimes regarded as 'unacceptable'?

- What is the difference between suppressing anger and not throwing the bricks in frustration? Is it appropriate to encourage children to keep a 'stiff upper lip' in response to difficulties?

- If we deny children opportunities to express in their play the violent images they see in the media, how else are they going to try to interpret what they see and hear?

- To what extent should early years, practitioners be politically astute and aware?

Supporting thinking

There are some key principles that underpin the practice in the 'helicopter technique'. A few are examined below, with numbered points taken directly from the story, in order to understand how this practitioner's approach supports the belief that children have an entitlement to express feelings and concerns – feelings of anger, frustration, fear, sadness or distress. Sometimes those feelings will spring from acts of violence.

Children must have opportunities to express these emotions, whilst also respecting the rights of others not to be subjected to violence.

1. 'the child knew the technique well'

This activity occurred because both children and adults understood the ways in which story-telling works. The teacher's knowledge of child development ensured she understood the growth of their powers of 'attention, concentration, memory, thinking, learning and language' (Wood 1998: 16). In promoting children's metacognition, the teacher was able to maximise opportunities for them to articulate their own ideas, likes and dislikes. They were able to be spontaneous and responsive to the purposeful activities provided by the teacher (Adams and Moyles 2001).

2. 'But I trusted the child'

The adult trusted the children and showed this by being prepared to allow the child to take the lead in the the story acting. Griffiths and Davies (1995: 36) describe how they set out to increase feelings of trust in their work with children in order to establish and improve attitudes of fairness in their classroom. One of the writers records:

> *I particularly felt it important to get to know the children and to explore what was happening in my class. I therefore decided to keep a diary over the first few weeks of the term to observe the class and review any problems that were occurring.*

Griffiths and Davies (ibid) explain that the teacher worked in partnership with the children to establish ground-rules, skills, trust and security, and began to explore what would help them to talk together as a class. Analysis of the children's ideas and contributions to the exploration revealed that, whilst they knew generally what was involved in discussing things, they did not have enough experience of discussion in practice.

Further negotiations resulted in the creation of a class list entitled 'What helps discussion take place'. The teacher was able to use this as an aid to build on these skills by exploring real issues with the children. Griffiths adds, 'Through this the children would see that we really do take note of what they say … and that we respect confidences' (ibid: 44).

3. 'I felt unsure, out of my depth'

The adult is engaged in on-going reflection and deliberation, confronting her own 'not-knowing'. It has been found that acknowledging insecurities

– the state of not knowing – is critical in developing a reflective approach to practice (Adams 2001; Dahlberg et al. 1999).

A willingness to acknowledge issues of practice helps to surface and articulate some of its related issues. This adult is unsure, yet her practice is based on a sound knowledge of child development. She has a clear understanding of children's metacognition and a confidence and trust in children's ability to make decisions. In order to clarify her understanding she turns to the children and asks them to elaborate – 'I'm curious to know why you are so keen to do that story again'.

4. 'I was surprised'

The teacher respects children's entitlement to make decisions and have ownership of their learning (Wood 1998). In the face of uncertainty, the practitioner continues to ensure that practice remains underpinned by a principle that children are entitled to opportunities to make decisions about aspects of their own learning. Without the teacher's dedication to this principle, it is unlikely that the children would have taken the opportunity to express their concerns about the effects of the explosions, the role of the firemen and the impact of such violence on their lives.

Wadsworth (1996) states that children bring to school many ideas and concepts which they wish to explore. It is the teacher's responsibility to identify the sources of interests that motivate children in order to promote further curiosity. This responsibility will extend to a degree of political awareness, so that informed interpretations may be made about children's play. Wadsworth continues (ibid: 151):

> When children communicate a strong interest in something, they are often communicating to us as parents or teachers that the area of interest has generated cognitive conflict for them. It is of value in education to legitimise and make productive use of interests. Interests can be viewed as part of the child's emerging lesson plans for their personal development. Although children's interests and teachers' curriculum goals rarely mesh neatly, creative, autonomous teachers can find ways to allow [children] to pursue their interests and accomplish the teachers' goals as well.

To return to the focus of this publication, observing and responding to children's interests or areas of 'cognitive conflict' provides teachers with opportunities to understand and to promote further aspects of personal development. The principles illustrated in this Focus can be applied to children's representations of violent acts, such as those we have been discussing in previous sections.

In the helicopter technique, the practitioner presents one way of helping children to act out emerging concerns through creating a forum for open discussion with them.

5. 'because where I was confused, the child was right. She knew we had tapped into something really powerful'

Throughout this story, there is evidence of the teacher's respect for young learners. This belief is retained even when the teacher is confused by the children's unpredictable responses. After the story acting had finished, she allowed a period of quiet reflection. The children were provided with an opportunity to consider their own responses to the powerful experience of story acting.

The teacher's practice is characterised by humility, which ensures she listens to, and hears the child's request to 'do it again'. She acknowledges that adults do not often let children tap into powerful emotions and responses – to explore fears and confront insecurities. However, the teacher's confidence in her methods and approach enables her to empower the children so that they can articulate their fears and act them out in a stress-free way.

Supporting practice

A critical feature of this practitioner's methodology is that it is underpinned by a respect for young children and informed by the ways in which children learn. This meant that she did not try to protect them from discussing sensitive issues. We are not suggesting that the only way – or even the best way – of responding to children's representations of cultural violence is simply to invite one child to tell a story to the class. However, the foundation principles and the sensitive and informed way in which children explored their fears provide a model for further consideration and application. By building on children's learning styles and by providing appropriate structures, founded on trust and openness, for children to use to work through their concerns, the practitioner was able to help children to be comfortable in expressing their fears.

The key practical points of this Focus are:

1. The children:

    - understood what was expected of them.

    - knew how to story-tell.

2. The practitioner:

    - trusted the children.

    - engaged in critical reflection.

    - was not afraid to 'let go' and be surprised by children's responses.

    - respected children's decisions.

    - did not protect the children from reality, but aimed to develop strategies to help them cope with difficult issues.

Focus Twelve

Cultural violence is all pervasive and influences practitioners' constructs of childhood and the role they have in supporting children's development and learning.

Introduction

This final focus point is really an all-embracing one: cultural violence is very pervasive. It invades and affects all aspects of our lives and those of the children with whom we work and play. How we view children from different cultural and racial backgrounds will in turn affect the way we support their development and learning.

A belief in the whole child – something dear to the heart of all practitioners – means accepting children for whom they are, and accepting too the families and communities from which they come. But the 'whole child', as we see in the case study below, is a very complex individual.

Case study Habib, Rupa and Tasmin (all aged 5 years) are playing in the home area. Habib (a Muslim child) has cordoned off the doorway of this three-sided structure with chairs and large plastic bricks, and has used this to 'imprison' Rupa and Tasmin.

'You are my hostages' Habib says. 'I'm going to kill you if you don't pay me a million dollars.' The two girls squeal and feign fear. Rupa says, 'My daddy will come and help me – he'll get us out.'

'Only if he pays me lots and lots of money,' says Habib. 'Or I'll cut you up in pieces and throw you away!' The play continues for a further few minutes until Tasmin starts to cry.

'I don't like you,' she says to Habib. 'I don't want to play any more.' 'Don't worry,' says Habib, 'It's only a game.' But Tasmin is clearly getting more and more upset.

Rupa takes the situation in hand. 'Stop it, Habib, please. We don't want to be prisoners any more.'

'It's OK,' says Habib, 'I'm only 'tending.'

Rupa cuddles Tasmin whilst Habib takes down the barricade and releases his two hostages. He touches both the girls gently as they walk by. 'It'll be all right,' he says.

Questions for practitioners

• Do you think that this play reflects situations children might have seen recently on television?

• How do you feel about the way the 'hostages' handled this situation?

- How do you feel about the way the 'captor' handled this situation?

- Should this kind of play be permitted in settings? If so, why? If not, why not?

- If you had observed children in your setting playing in this way, how would you have reacted?

- How do you respond to the way Rupa reacted to her friend being upset? How do you respond to Habib taking down the barricades?

- What is the role of the adult in this play? Should the hostage situation have been allowed? At what point might the practitioner have intervened or interacted?

Support for thinking and practice

In this final section we deviate from the general pattern. We have offered support for thinking about the issues in each of the previous focus points. In this the final focus, we will try to draw together all the previous sections and show how this case study exemplifies the kind of practice – and reflection on practice – we have discussed and advocated throughout.

The three key areas of media, practitioners and children are all well represented. Whilst the case study does not represent any particular event, it is clear that many hostage situations have been featured on television and in other media over the last few years. The aftermath of the Iraq war and images from Guantanamo Bay are just two such contexts. Imprisonment has been a recurring theme of children's play since we were children ourselves! But now it appears to take on a different resonance. The example of chopping people into pieces in this case study suggests new levels of violence coming from children's exposure to images arising from recent events. This is a matter which practitioners need to consider and address.

Gender issues are also apparent in this case study. The captor demonstrates male power over female captives (Skelton 2001). The girls suitably 'squeal' and look to another male (father) for support. However, Habib shows a gentle side to his nature when he realises that Tamsin is upset and agrees to release her and her friend.

We know that children of this age can show considerable sophistication, as does Rupa in being able to empathasise with Tasmin's distress. She also shows well-honed personal skills and commendable assertiveness in being able to tell Habib to stop pursuing the hostage situation so that Tasmin can be 'freed'. Being able to say 'enough is enough' and extricate oneself from an unhappy situation shows Rupa's ability to create her own boundaries and rules. Not only can she do this for herself, but she is able to do this for her friend, Tasmin. The fact that she can then negotiate with another child from a different racial background (Habib) and secure what she is seeking (release from the hostage situation), would leave many politicians feeling inadequate!

Many of the focus points we have discussed previously are encapsulated in this case study. We do not get to know immediately how the adult perceived this situation, or what preceded this incident in terms of adult input. We can perhaps conjecture that the children had been given plenty of opportunity to discuss various violent situations and how to handle them – a process we have been advocating throughout. Children had clearly learned empathy with each other's feelings and how to recognise real distress. Rupa sees the effect the play is having on Tasmin and inter- venes. When Habib's attention is drawn to the way the play is upsetting Rupa he immediately stops. They were also able to take account of each other's perspectives. Habib was ready to admit that he was only pretending and that everything would be 'alright', presumably meaning that the upset Tasmin could once more feel free and comfortable and be his friend.

It is always difficult to interpret children's actions and reactions, but one has the duty to make a good guess in order to support each child in an holistic way. While it would appear that these children are learning to cope well with their own emotional responses to situations, the practitioner needs to be alert to why Tasmin, in this case, is distressed.

Images of Violence

After reading this case study, one colleague asked, 'Why did the practitioner allow the children to take their play to the point where Tasmin was clearly so upset?' We raised this very point ourselves with the practitioner (June). She told us that she wanted to see how far the children were able to conduct their own negotiations. She had been doing a lot of work with the children during group and circle time discussing emotions by, for example, using books like 'Angry Arthur' (Oram 1993) and persona dolls to act out events which have a racial element, and which had emerged in this very multi-cultural classroom. She had been pleased to see that the majority of children were prepared to tell others if they found actions or words distressing, threatening or uncomfortable. Tasmin is usually one of these children but her distress on this occasion was a puzzle to June, who will now want to observe the child in a range of activities and try, when appropriate, to talk with her.

In June's setting the differentiation between reality and fantasy has already been explored with children. All three children in the case study were happy at first with the hostage play scenario. It was clearly something they had seen or heard, perhaps during the television news, and they wanted to experiment with the experience of capturing and being captive. However, something, perhaps the threat of physical harm, triggered fear and concern in Tasmin which was immediately recognised and dealt with by Rupa. Far from being 'desensitised' by the media (as we suggested in Focus One), these children are able to take what they see and play with the ideas. The practitioner has helped them to acquire skills that enable them to cope, mostly effectively, with different emotions (Focus Two).

While Habib threatened (playful) violence, he acknowledged that he was only pretending. He recognised the differences between reality and fantasy (Focus Three) as well as the distress of his companions. June and her colleagues have thought deeply about racial issues and cultural violence, and discussed strategies for handling challenging situations themselves and with the children (Focus Four). It has been vital for June and the other practitioners to understand the diversity within their local community and to develop policies and practices which reflect the whole range of different cultures, races and ethnic groups represented in the setting (Focus Five). Their policy is to make notes on and discuss all specific incidents, like the hostage situation in this case study, at weekly staff meetings. While June is an experienced member of staff, others may need the focus of a whole staff meeting to think through ways in which they might have handled the play and the upset caused to Tasmin.

This will probably involve revisiting the equal opportunities policy (see Focus Six). The related issue of protecting the rights of all involved in a particular situation like the hostage play has, in this case, been allotted to the children, who cope well between the three of them in addressing Tasmin's concerns (see Focus Seven). June's later discussion with the three children and others who had been peripheral to the play, emphasised the need for children to tell others when situations make them unhappy or worried, rather than ignore them. Children have learned to trust June, as she has continually given them time and space to talk – or not – about their feelings. They know they will receive a 'sympathetic ear' and be given opportunities to play out their fears (see Focus Eight).

Habib (Muslim), Rupa (Hindu) and Tasmin (Afro-Caribbean) are children of different faiths, cultures and ethnic groups. Whilst they have been brought up very differently, each has learned to empathise with the feelings of others and to respond with understanding and compassion. This suggests that the staff in the setting have focussed on the similarities between children rather than on differences (see Focus Nine). The respect given to each child has led to them all knowing that they can play out situations they have seen on television in a secure environment and talk about their feelings and responses (see Focus Ten). Tasmin knew that when she expressed her fears others would listen and respond, and the situation could be resolved (see Focus Eleven).

How June and her colleagues chose to deal with activities such as the hostage play shows that they recognise the influence that the media and cultural violence have on children's learning and development. It also

Images of Violence

shows that they have undertaken significant reflection in order to apply their thoughts to their practice.

Tailpiece

This book has been written in response to the incessant, unrelenting coverage and constantly repeated images of violence that have impacted on children's play and psyche following September 11th. In the Introduction we asked: Are we able to bring informed pedagogical understanding to the consideration of what children make of the violent images with which they are now surrounded in everyday life? We invited you to think about your response to Joseph's model of the twin towers and your feelings towards it. We then examined some of the concerns and dilemmas about perceptions of violence and race which face practitioners, particularly in the wake of the kind of violent events associated with September 11th 2001, and those which have followed. This publication is intended to help staff in settings and schools to consider the importance of examining their own knowledge, understanding and feelings in order to support children and families more effectively. This includes taking account of the many children and families in settings who have experienced acts of violence in their own countries of origin and have come to this country as refugees.

The whole notion of September 11th being the starting point for our discussion reflects our own Eurocentric attitudes and response. This is unavoidable. However, we acknowledge the truth that children everywhere in the world have suffered and are suffering from cultural and racial violence and vast inequalities. We acknowledge that deaths from the violence in the Sudan or Rwanda dwarf those in New York, Madrid or Bali. We also know that while we enjoy our affluent, comfortable world, thousands of children die from hunger every day, and that this is another, hideous type of violence. It seems to us that adults and children are confronted with double standards when it comes to global terrorism. The invasion of Iraq was apparently an act to be celebrated by politicians and the media, but invasion of other people's nations through terrorism is not acceptable. As we said in the introduction, this is a highly complex area.

It is confusing enough for adults, so it is no wonder that children find difficulties and problems.

In a short publication we have had to accept that we are touching only the tip of a very large iceberg. Nevertheless, we feel it important to start somewhere on a discussion of important issues that have been, and are, challenging many people who work with children. Through using authentic case studies, it has been possible to illustrate the processes of pedagogical reasoning that are occurring in schools and settings where practitioners are attempting to find a way of helping children to cope with the violent images they encounter and work through their feelings of vulnerability and insecurity. Responding to the case studies presented here has drawn on many professional skills and processes. In considering the dilemmas facing the twelve practitioners whose work is discussed, we have engaged in reflective analysis, deliberation, confrontation and interpretation of children's behaviours. This is a luxury which is not always available in schools and settings, where practitioners are often required to respond at once to children's behaviours.

We hope that the arguments we have put forward will support readers in their personal engagement with the topics we have discussed, and in the many professional decisions they have to make in the course of daily confrontations with children's representations of violence. We suggest that all practitioners need to reflect on and consider the impact of global terrorism and its associated images on the children in their care. Perhaps this publication may serve as a catalyst for thinking. Day proposes (1999: 221) that:

> *Continuing professional development is essential if teachers [practitioners] are to remain up-to-date in their knowledge of the curriculum, wise in their actions and use of a repertoire of pedagogical skills … [and] committed and enthusiastic about their work.*

Continuing professional development demands that practitioners engage not only with practice but with deeper issues. These include the examination of society's construct of childhood and addressing concerns of which many practitioners may be unaware, that 'their behaviour may be discriminating in effect, if not in intent' (Biggs and Edwards 1992: 162). Nowadays, there is ample support for thinking about equality, race and cultural issues. For example, The MacPherson Report (1999), the Race Relations (Amendment) Act 2000, The Human Rights Act (1998) and the OFSTED Framework for Educational Inclusion (2000). All institutions are required by law to be aware of the possibility of - and to take steps to avoid - institutional racism. All practitioners must have regard to this in approaching cultural and racial violence.

We would not try to simplify the complex nature of critical reflection. It is challenging and difficult. We offer as an aid the following six points, which deconstruct some of the key processes that have been used during the discussions of each of the focus points (Mailhos 1999). It sets out the stages of thinking by which practitioners can respond to the issues raised in this publication

1. Identifying and selecting appropriate knowledge

Ensuring you are aware of the situation.

Asking: What do I need to understand about this situation / background / context?

2. Identifying and selecting appropriate materials

Providing resources or toys that relate to the issue, e.g. guns.

Asking: What might the children be doing?

3. Identifying learning situations

Encouraging feelings of responsibility, e.g. by providing hospital resources to help children care for their patients or 'victims'.

Asking: What do I want the children to learn?

4. Assessing learning episodes

Planning for time to observe and interpret children's responses.

Asking: What have the children learned from this experience?

5. Conceptualising teaching episodes

Relating this to the policy and curriculum of the school or setting.

Asking: What dispositions, values and attitudes have children learned?

6. Transfer learning to new teaching situations

Planning to promote children's skills and development.

Asking: What will I need to teach next?

Ricard-Fersing (1999) concludes that in practice reflexivity is characterised by dignity and the complexity of its actions. Throughout this publication, the complexity of educational analysis has been very apparent. We have all been challenged by the aftermath of September 11th and other acts of violence and war.

The evidence from the practitioners who have contributed their stories here suggests that pedagogical reasoning honours and respects children's entitlement to inclusion, equality and dignity. This is something that, in itself, is worthy of reflection.

We have emphasised in this book the challenges of facing up to dealing with the ways children respond to images of violence. We have considered examples of their representations of violence and the terrorism and racism which seem to be growing elements. We have also emphasised the vital role of the practitioners in facing, handling and understanding the perspectives of children, their families and communities; and, perhaps even more importantly, in understanding themselves and their own perspectives and responses.

It seems appropriate to leave the final words to a practitioner. She is struggling to come to terms with the issues with which this book is concerned, and is working her way towards her own rationale.

In many ways, living and working in a majority white, middle class suburban area, I feel cocooned from many aspects of cultural violence. We have our own different sets of problems of course, but it's been hard knowing what to do, when bits of racist and aggressive language have crept into the playground and even my classroom, especially since September 11th.

Looking back, I allowed myself to be naïve: you know, there was never any urgency to respond to the unpleasant things that happen in other villages, towns or cities. I'm not a very political person or anything like that, but now I know and understand more about the racial and cultural tensions that pervade so much of our society. I feel better able to cope with it really. I've also taken time to research other cultures, so I'm much better informed about the ways in which society has developed and been enriched by additional traditions. I used to be a bit of an ostrich – happy to keep my head in the sand because it didn't really bother me. But now, well, you know things change. I know more, understand more and think I'm a more responsive, informed and reflective teacher because of it. At least I don't shy away from my responsibilities. I'm more politically aware and do try to be professional and objective in my reasoning.

In some ways, working in an all white school it's hard to ensure our children learn to respect each other, especially children whose culture is different from that within our own community. Now I'm better informed, I can see the underlying issues of tolerance, respect, acknowledging differences and similarities – it's all there, waiting to be challenged and acted upon.

References & Bibliography ■

These references are sub-divided into four sections to enable readers to decide which books are most appropriate for their purposes.

The four sections are:

> *1. Supporting practice*   *2. Supporting thinking*
>
> *3. Supporting management*   *4. Supporting research*

If you wish to read to support your everyday practice, then the first section 'Supporting Practice' contains a number of very useful and readable books and articles for this purpose. 'Supporting Thinking', on the other hand, contains books and papers for those who want to reflect more deeply on the issues raised in this publication. If you have a senior management role, then 'Supporting Management' contains books and articles to support that role. Those pursuing research, either as advanced studies students or as researchers, will find the final section useful. Of course there are many overlaps in the four sections and readers should bear this in mind.

Supporting Practice

Askew, S. and Ross, C. (1988) Boys Don't Cry: boys and sexism in education. Milton Keynes: Open University Press.

Bagnall, D. (2000) Born to be Wired. The Bulletin, 15th August.

Baig, R. with Lane, J. (2003) Building Bridges for our Future: this way forward through times of terror and war. London: EYTARN (Early Years Trainers Anti-Racist Network).

Biggs, A. and Edwards, V. (1992) 'I treat them all the same' Teacher-Pupil Talk in Multi-ethnic Classrooms. Language and Education. 5(2), 161-176.

Blurton Jones, N. (1972) Categories of Child-Child Interaction. In Blurton Jones, N. (ed.) Ethological Studies of Child Behaviour. 24, 97-127.

Broadhead, P. (2004) Early Years Play and Learning: Developing Social Skills and Co-operation. London: Routledge Falmer.

Broadhead, P. (1992) 'Play-fighting, play or fighting? – from parallel to co-operative play in the pre-school. Early Years. 13(1), 45-49.

Bruce, T. (1992) Time to Play in early childhood education. London: Hodder and Stoughton.

Carlsson-Paige, N. and Levin, D. (1990) Who's Calling the Shots? How to respond effectively to children's fascination with war play and war toys. Philadelphia: New Society Publishers.

DfEE/QCA (2000) Curriculum Guidance for the Foundation Stage. London: DfES/QCA.

Dunn, J. and Hughes, C. (2001) "I got some swords and you're dead!" Violent fantasy, antisocial behaviour, friendship and moral sensibility in young children. Child Development. 72, 491-505.

Graddol, D. and Swann, J. (1989) Gender Voices. Cambridge: Cambridge University Press.

Heaslip, P. (1994) Making play work in the classroom. In Moyles, J. (ed.) The Excellence of Play Buckingham: Open University Press.

Holland, P. (2003) We don't play guns here: War, weapon and superhero play in the early years. Maidenhead: Open University Press.

Hyder, T. (in press) War, Conflict and Play. Buckingham: Open University Press.

Kerr, J. (2002) Goodbye, Mog. New York: Collins.

Kitson, N. (1995) 'Please Miss Alexander: will you be the robber?' Fantasy play: a case for adult intervention. In Moyles, J. (ed) The Excellence of Play. Buckingham: Open University Press.

Lane, J. (1999) Action for Racial Equality in the Early Years: understanding the past, thinking about the present, planning for the future. London: EYTARN.

Oram, H. (1993) Angry Arthur. London: Red Fox.

McKee, D. (1980) Not Now Bernard. London: Red Fox.

McNaughton, G. (2000) Rethinking Gender in Early Childhood Education. London: Paul Chapman.

Mollie, C. (2001) Building a peaceful school: strategies and interventions for primary schools. Tamworth: NASEN

Moyles, J, (1989) Just Playing? The Role and Status of Play in Early Childhood Education. Milton Keynes: Open University Press.

Moyles, J. (Ed) (1994) The Excellence of Play. Buckingham: Open University Press

Moyles, J. and Adams, S. (2001) StEPs: Statements of Entitlement to Play. Buckingham: Open University Press.

Moyles, J. (2002) Beginning Teaching: Beginning Learning in Primary Education (2nd edn) Buckingham: Open University Press.

Moyles, J., Adams, S. and Musgrove, A. (2002) SPEEL: Study of Pedagogical Effectiveness in Early Learning. London: DfES. Report No: 363.

Moyles, J. and Musgrove, A. (2003) EEPES (EY) Essex Effective Pedagogy Evaluation Scheme (Early Years). Research Report. Chelmsford APU/Essex County Council.

Nicholls, J. and Cockroft, J. (2002) Billywise. London: Bloomsbury.

Oram, H. and Kitamura, S. (1993) Angry Arthur. London: Red Fox.

O'Regan, M. (2000) Children's Programmes on TV. The Media Report 3. August. www.abc.net.au/rn/talks/8.30/mediarpt/stories/sl159007.htm

Paley, V. (1986) Boys and Girls: superheroes in the doll corner. University of Chicago Press.

Paley, V. (1991) The Boy Who Would be a Helicopter. London: Harvard University Press.

Paley, V. (1997) The Girl with the Brown Crayon. London: Harvard University Press.

Paley, V. (1999) The Kindness of Children. London: Harvard University Press.

Radunsky, V. (2003) Mannekin Pis. London: Walker Books.

Root, P. (2002) Big Mama Makes the World. London: Walker Books.

Roberts, R. (1995) Self-esteem and Successful Early Learning. London: Hodder and Stoughton.

Ross, C. and Browne, N. (1993) Girls as Constructors in the Early Years: Promoting Equal Opportunities in maths, science and technology. Stoke-on-Trent: Trentham Books.

Sayeed, Z. and Guerin, S. (2000) Early Years Play: A Happy Medium for Assessment and Intervention. London: David Fulton.

Smith, P.K. and Lewis, K. (1985) Rough and Tumble Play, Fighting and Chasing in Nursery School Children. Ethnology and Sociology. 6, 175-181.

Suschitzky, W. (1995) It's not fair! Equal opportunities in practice. In Moyles, J. (ed) Beginning Teaching: Beginning Learning in Primary Education. Buckingham: Open University Press.

Suschitzky, W. and Chapman, J. (1998) Valued Children: Informed Teaching. Buckingham: Open University Press.

Tephly, J. (1985) Young children's understanding of war and peace. Early Child Development and Care. 20(4), 271-285.

Webster-Stratton, C. (1999) How to Promote Children's Social and Emotional Competence. London: Paul Chapman.

Images of Violence

Supporting thinking

Adams, S., Alexander, E., Drummond, M-J. and Moyles, J. (2004) Inside the Foundation Stage: Recreating the Reception Year. Report on research commissioned by the Association of Teachers and Lecturers: London.

Alibhai, Y. (1987) The Child Racists. New Society, 82(1301), 13-15.

Aries, P. (1962) Centuries of Childhood. New York: Jonathan Cape.

Arnot, M., David, M. and Weiner, G. (1999) Closing the Gender Gap: post-war education and social change. Cambridge: Polity Press.

Brittan, A. (1989) Masculinity and Power. Oxford: Basil Blackwell.

Brah, A. and Minhas, R. (1988) Structural racism or cultural difference: Schooling for Asian girls. In Woodhouse, M. and McGrath, A. (eds.) Family, School and Society. London: Hodder and Stoughton.

Brown, D. (1994) Play, the playground and the culture of childhood. In Moyles, J. The Excellence of Play Buckingham: Open University Press

Connor, K. (1989) Aggression: Is it in the eye of the beholder? Play and Culture. 2, 213–217.

David, T. (ed) (1999) Working Together for Young Children. London: Routledge

Erricker, C. (1998) Journeys through the heart: the effect of death, loss and conflict on children's worldviews. Journal of Beliefs and Values. 19(1), 107-118.

Farrell, A., Taylor, C. Tennent, L. and Gahan, D. (1999) Listening to Children: a study of child and family services. Early Years: Journal on International Research and Development. 22(1), 17-38.

Gipps, C., McCallum, B. and Hargreaves, E. (2000) What Makes a Good Primary School Teacher? Expert Classroom Strategies London: Routledge/Falmer.

Glauser, B. (1997) Street Children: Deconstructing a Construct. In James, A. and Prout, A. (1997) Constructing and Reconstructing Childhood. London: Falmer Press.

Goldstein, J. (ed) Toys, Play and Child Development. Cambridge: Cambridge University Press.

Haring, Keith (1997) I Wish I Didn't Have to Sleep, London: Prestel.

Jacobson, M. and Mazur, L. (1995) Marketing Madness: A Survival Guide for a Consumer Society. Boulder CO: Westview Press.

James, A. and Prout, A. (1997) Constructing and Reconstructing Childhood. London: Falmer Press.

Kantor, R., Elgas, P., and Fernie, D. Cultural knowledge and social competence within a preschool peer-culture group. In Woodhead, M., Faulkner, D. and Littleton, K. Cultural Worlds of Childhood. London: Routledge.

Katch, J. (2001) Under Deadman's Skin: Discovering the Meaning of Children's Play. Boston: Beacon Press.

Kenway, J. and Bullen, E. (2001) Consuming Children: Education, Entertainment, Advertising Buckingham: Open University Press.

Klerfelt, A. (2004) Ban the computer, or make it a storytelling machine. bridging the gap between the children's media culture and pre-school. Scandinavian Journal of Educational Research 48(1), 73–93.

Kitzinger, J. (1997) Who are you kidding? Children, Power and the Struggle against Sexual Abuse In James, A. and Prout, A. (1997) Constructing and Reconstructing Childhood. London: Falmer Press.

Kohlberg, L. (1985) The Psychology of Moral Development. New York: Harper and Row.

Mackay, H. (1997) Generations: Baby Boomers, Their Parents and Their Children. Sydney: Pan Macmillan.

Moyles, J, Hargreaves, L., Merry, R., Paterson, A. and Esarte-Sarries, V. (2003) Interactive Teaching in the Primary School: Digging Deeper into Meanings. Buckingham: Open University Press.

Opie, I. (1993) The People in the Playground. Oxford: Oxford University Press.

Siraj-Blatchford, I. (ed). (1993) Race, Gender and the Education of Teachers. Buckingham: Open University Press.

Skelton, C. (2001) Schooling the Boys: Masculinities and Primary Education. Buckingham: Open University Press.

Smith, P. K. (1994) The war play debate. In Goldstein, J. (ed) Toys, Play and Child Development. Cambridge: Cambridge University Press.

Smith, P. K. (2004a) Social and pretend play in children. In Pellegrini, A. and Smith, P. K. (eds.) Play in humans and apes. Mahwah, N.J. Erlbaum.

Smith, P. K. (2004b) Play: Types and Functions in Human Development. In, Ellis. B. and Bjorklund, D. (eds.) Origins of the Social Mind: Evolutionary Psychology and Child Development. New York: Guilford Publications.

Sutton-Smith, B. (1988) War toys and childhood aggression. Play and Culture. 1, 57-69.

Wilson, J. (1985) First Steps in Moral Education: Understanding and using reason. In Modgil, S. and Modgil, C. (eds.) Lawrence Kohlberg: Consensus and Controversy. Lewes: Falmer Press.

Wood, D. (1998) How Children Think and Learn. Oxford.

Wood, D. (1998) Aspects of Teaching and Learning. In Cultural Worlds of Childhood. Woodhead, M., Faulkner, D. and Littleton, K. London: Routledge.

Supporting management

Boyden, J. (1997) Childhood and Policymakers: A Comparative Perspective on the Globalisation of Childhood. In James, A. and Prout, A. (1997) Constructing and Reconstructing Childhood London: Falmer Press.

Bruce, T. and Meggitt, C. (1999) Child Care and Education. London: Hodder and Stoughton.

Commission on Children and Violence (1995) Children and Violence. London: Calouste Gulbenkian Foundation.

Dahlberg, G., Moss, P. and Pence, A. (1999) Beyond Quality in Early Childhood Education and Care. London: Falmer Press.

Day, C. (1999) Professional Development and Reflective Practice Purposes, Processes and Partnerships. Pedagogy, Culture and Practice. 7(2), 221-234.

Dunn, J. (1998) Young children's Understanding of other people In Woodhead, M., Faulkner, D. and Littleton, K. (eds.) Cultural Worlds of Early Childhood. London: Routledge in association with The Open University.

Escobar-Ortloff, L. and Ortloff, W. (2003) A Cultural Change for School Administrators. Intercultural Education. 14(3), 255–261.

EYTARN (Early Years Trainers Anti-Racist Network) (1995) A Policy for Excellence: developing a policy for equality in early years settings. London: EYTARN. (see website for other refs: www.earlyyearsequality.org.uk)

Great Britain Parliament House (1998) Human Rights Act, 1998 (Public General Acts - Elizabeth II). London: The Stationery Office.

Griffiths, M. and Davies, C. (1995) In Fairness to Children. London: David Fulton.

Holland, P. (2000) Take the Toys from the Boys? An examination of the genesis of policy and the appropriateness of adult perspective in the area of war, weapon and superhero play. Children's Social and Economics Education. 4(2), 92-107.

Kelly, L. and Mullander, A. (2000) Complexities and contradictions: living with domestic violence and the UN Convention on Children's Rights. International Journal of Children's Rights. 8, 229-241.

MacPherson, W. (1999) The Stephen Lawrence Inquiry. London: The Stationery Office

Office for Standards in Education (2000) Evaluating Educational Inclusion: Guidance for Inspectors and Schools. London: OfSTED

Qualifications and Curriculum Authority (2000) Curriculum Guidance for the Foundation Stage. London: DfEE.

Rinaldi, C. (1994) Observation and documentation. Paper given at the Research Conference at Reggio Emilia. June 1995.

Supporting research

Adams, S. (2001) An Investigation of the Deconstruction and Reconstruction Processes within the Context of Reflective Pedagogical Practice and within the Content of Play. University of Leicester. Unpublished Doctoral Thesis.

Ansari, H. (2002) The Working Mosque: A case study of Muslim engagement with British Society since 1889. Immigrants and Minorities. 21(3), 1-22.

Arber, R. (2003) The ambivalence of otherness: the manifestation of 'whiteness' in an Australian school. Journal of Intercultural Studies. 24(3), 289–305.

Connolly, P. (1998) Racism, gender identities and young children: Social relations in a multi-ethnic primary school. London: Routledge.

Costabile, A., Smith, P., Matheson, L., Aston, J., Hunter, T. and Coulton, M. (1991) Cross-national comparison of how children distinguish serious and playful fighting. Developmental Psychology. 27(5), 881-887.

Day, C., Fernandez, A., Hauge, T. and Møller J. (Eds.) (2000) The Life and Work of Teachers: International Perspective in Changing Times. London: Falmer Press.

DeWitt, S. (2003) Multicultural Democracy and Inquiry Pedagogy. Intercultural Education. 14(3), 279–290.

Edleson, J. (1999) Children's Witnessing of Adult Domestic Violence. Journal of Interpersonal-Violence. 14(8), 839-870.

Giavrimis, P., Konstantinou, E. Hatzichristou, C. (2003) Dimensions of immigrant students' adaptation in the Greek schools: self-concept and coping strategies. Intercultural Education. 14(4), 423–434.

Grossman, D., Neckerman, H., Koepsell, T., Liu, P., Asher, K., Beland, K., Frey, K. and Rivara, F. (1997) Effectiveness of a violence prevention curriculum among children in elementary school. Journal of American Medical Association. 277, 1605-1611.

Herr, K. (1999) Private power and privileged education: deconstructing institutionalised racism. International Journal of Inclusive Education. 3(2), 111–129.

Holland, P. (1999) Is Zero Tolerance Intolerant? Early Childhood Practice. 1(1), Spring, 65-72.

Husu, J. (2003) Constructing teachers' knowledge from their pedagogical practices - analyzing narratives of and in action. Paper presented at the 11th Biennial Conference of the International Study Association on Teachers and Teaching (ISATT), Leiden, The Netherlands: 27 June-1 July 2003.

Jones, L. (2001) Trying to Break Bad Habits by Engaging with Poststructuralist Theories. Early Years Journal of Reseach and Development. 21(1), 25–32.

Kohlberg, L. (1985) Consensus and Controversy. Lewes: Falmer Press.

Ladd, G. (1981) Effectiveness of a social learning method of enhancing children's social interaction and peer acceptance. Child Development. 52(1), 171-178.

Mailhos, M. (1999) Reflective Practice and the Development of Pedagogical Reasoning. Pedagogy, Culture and Society. 7(2), 329-360.

Martens, B. and Meller, P. (1990) The application of behavioural principles to educational settings. In Gutkin, T. and Reynolds, C. (eds.) Handbook of School Psychology. New York: Wiley.

Moyles, J., Adams, S. and Musgrove, A. (2002) Study of Pedagogical Effectiveness in Early Learning. Paper presented at British Educational Research Association Conference. University of Exeter, September.

Much, N. and Shweder, R. (1979) Speaking of Rules: the analysis of culture in breach. In Damon, W. (ed.) New Directions for Child Development: Moral Development 2. San Francisco, California: Jossey-Bass.

Nsamenang, A. and Lamb, M. (1998) Socialisation of Nso children in the Bamenda Grassfields of the Northwest Cameroon. In Woodhead, M., Faulkner, D. and Littleton, K. (eds.) Cultural Worlds of Early Childhood. London: Routledge in association with The Open University.

O'Donnell, D., Schwab-Stone, M. and Moyeed, A. (2002) Family, School and Community: Multidimensional Resilience in Urban Children exposed to community violence. Child Development. 73(4), 1265–1282.

Orpinas, P., Murray, M. and Kelder, S. (1999) Parental influences on students' aggressive behaviours and weapon carrying. Health Education and Behaviour. 26(6), 774-787.

Punamaki, R. and Pijhakki, T. Determinants and Effectiveness of Children Coping with Political Violence. International Journal of Behavioural Development. 21(1), 349-370.

ky, L. (1978) Mind in Society. Cambridge, Mass: Harvard
sity Press.

orth, B. (1996) Piaget's Theory of Cognitive and Affective
pment. New York: Longman.

, A. (2004) The Child that Bombs Built. Studies in Conflict and
sm. 27(3), 159–168.

Ronen, T. (2002) Difficulties in Assessing Traumatic
Children. Journal of Loss and Trauma. 7(2), 87–106.

Schwartz, D., Lin, X., Holmes, J. (2003) Technologie
Intercultural Reflections. Intercultural Education. 1

Vygot
Unive

Wads
Devel

Watso
Terror

St John, P. (2003) The Songs Teachers Teach are
songs children sing: The boy who would be an a
Justice Review. 6(1), 47–53.

Taylor- Webb, P. (2001) Reflection and Reflective
improve pedagogy or ways to remain racist? Ra
Education. 4(3), 245–252.

Inside Out
ISBN 1 904187 27 7

by Sally Featherstone with Anne Cummings

How to plan and organise a range of role play situations, inside and out. Part 1 discusses why role play is important and Part 2 presents plans for a range of role play situations. There are ideas for materials, equipment and locations, including making the most of limited resources. Unlock your imagination and help your children to bring out what's inside!

Cooking Up A Story
ISBN 1 905019 00 9

by Mary Medlicott

A wonderful collection of stories and storytelling advice from a leading children's storyteller. The emphasis is on creativity and enjoyment – getting children engaged and using their imaginations. The sound, practical guidance for practitioners will help even the least confident to make the most of storytime. Delightfully illustrated in full colour by Martha Hardy.

The balance... is just right. I recommend this book...storytime is too important to be neglected.
Miranda Walker, Nursery World Magazine

Smooth Transitions
ISBN 1 904187 67 6

by Ros Bayley & Sally Featherstone

The tensions between Reception and KS1 have now been acknowledged. This book offers advice for teachers, practitioners, parents and managers on supporting children through the move from the Foundation Stage to Yr 1. Includes a special section on using new knowledge about how children learn.

This is brilliant! I want every infant teacher in Britain to have a copy.
Sue Palmer, Educational Consultant

Practical....accessible....invaluable. It will help you do what we all know is right for the children. Early Years Educator Magazine

Featherstone Education   PO Box 6350   Lutterworth LE17 6ZA
United Kingdom
T:+44 (0)185 888 1212   F:+44 (0)185 888 1360
sales@featherstone.uk.com
www.featherstone.uk.com